love island
ON PAPER

hamlyn

An Hachette UK Company
www.hachette.co.uk

First published in Great Britain in 2017 by Hamlyn, a division of
Octopus Publishing Group Ltd
Carmelite House, 50 Victoria Embankment, London EC4Y 0DZ
www.octopusbooks.co.uk
www.octopusbooksusa.com

Distributed in the US by Hachette Book Group, 1290 Avenue of the
Americas, 4th and 5th Floors, New York, NY 10104

Distributed in Canada by Canadian Manda Group, 664 Annette Street,
Toronto, Ontario, Canada M6S 2C8

ISBN 978 0 60063 541 3

A CIP catalogue record for this book is available from the British Library.

Printed and bound in Italy

10 9 8 7 6 5 4 3 2 1

Text by Steve Parry and Sabah Ahmed

Publishing Director Trevor Davies
Art Director Yasia Williams
Designer Abigail Read
Editor Zia Mattocks
Assistant Editor Ellie Corbett
Senior Production Manager Peter Hunt
Picture Research Manager Giulia Hetherington

love island
ON PAPER

The OFFICIAL Love Island Guide to

Grafting, Cracking on and Mugging off

Foreword by Caroline Flack
Preface by the voice of the show Iain Stirling

Written by
Steve Parry and Sabah Ahmed

hamlyn

Contents

Foreword
by Caroline Flack

Love Island is so much more than a job to me. I get as starstruck walking into that villa to announce a re-coupling or a dumping as I do going to any showbiz event. Islander or A-lister, I get the same giddy feeling. That's because I'm a superfan, or 'obsessive' as my friends call it, and I have been since day one, series one.

As well as being excited to see them in the flesh (oh, and what flesh!), as soon as I meet the Islanders for the first time I start to feel all protective of them. I want to take them under my wing and tell them that everything is going to be fine. More than fine! Everything in their lives is about to change dramatically and we're all in it together.

This year's show had the nation HOOKED and I can understand why. In the quest for human connection we got to know 32 new Islanders all looking for one thing – LOVE. OK, in some cases maybe more than one thing... Whether we were watching Marcel dishing out relationship advice, Olivia getting caught in the 'd**ksand' or 'Muggy' Mike making the two best entrances the villa has ever seen, we could see bits of ourselves and people we know in every single one of them.

This summer the show not only changed our daily routine, but it also changed the way we spoke. WhatsApp groups dedicated just to *Love Island* are now a common part of everyday communication. People leaving dinner parties early to get home by 9pm became a way of life. And if you don't have a 'type on paper', these days, then WHO EVEN ARE YOU????

I'm not someone who jumps into a relationship with both feet after one date. In fact, it usually takes me about a year to even admit 'I might like you a tiny little bit'. So what was great about this year's show was that everything had to be done in seven weeks – or, in Jess and Dom's case, two weeks. The Islanders were faced with having to talk about their feelings immediately. I can't help but think how much easier this actually makes a relationship. Perhaps we're missing a trick here – maybe we should all be living in luxury villas surrounded by potential lovers? Hmmmmm... Get rid of the cameras and the communal bedroom, and I'm in!

Whatever it is that makes you love the show as much as I do, we have to all agree that this year's Islanders played a strong game. Who knew that the gorgeous but timid Camilla would actually go on a 52-day journey of self-discovery, get her heart smashed into smithereens, but then walk out triumphant, with a ridiculously fit Calvin Klein model who can do no wrong? Who knew that there would be another villa full of five new girls? (I didn't – they wouldn't tell me because they thought I would explode!) Who knew that Chris and Olivia would last longer than a week in the outside world? And who knew that Kem and Amber would put the past behind them (the past being five weeks) and walk away hand in hand with £50,000 in their shared pocket and two pieces of coloured string tied sweetly around their loving wrists? I didn't, no one did. I predicted a different winning couple every single week, which shows just how close it was.

But the real winners in this whole awesome experience are us, the viewers. What a series! I still miss them all like crazy. My TV and Instagram feed feel empty without them. It was the perfect summer romance, never to be repeated. Until next year, of course – and I for one can't wait! Now, where's my passport...?

Preface *by Iain Stirling*

So here we are. *Love Island*'s only gone and got its own book. What a time to be alive! And I have been honoured with the task of writing a little introduction before the whole thing kicks right off.

So how do we go about this? Well, let's start with a 'thank you', and a big one at that. *Love Island* has changed my life and I will be forever indebted to the show, the team and you guys who watched it at home for that. But this isn't about how I now get free chips in my local kebab shop, it's about the show, *Love Island*. So, in the words of The Joker, 'Here. We. Go.'

This series of *Love Island* was more than just a TV show, it was a social phenomenon. It captured the imagination of a nation, and watercoolers up and down the UK were all the better for it. Talk of Brexit and Trump was swiftly replaced with chat about 'dumpings' and 'cracking on'. Not to mention Romford, which got its fair amount of air time. I always took great pleasure from the minutiae that people focused on during the show's summer run - Cash Hughes, Kem's unusual turns of phrase, Benny on Camera 2. It is all these little, seemingly insignificant extras that come together to create the *Love Island* world we choose to fill our summers with every year.

So what have I, Iain Stirling, learned from spending seven weeks on the Island of Love. Well, firstly, love is never simple. Nothing worth having is. Hopefully all your relationships won't be quite as fraught as Chris and Olivia's, but none will be plain sailing. You need to take the rough with the smooth and remind yourself constantly why you have chosen to let this person into your bizarre little world. Secondly, you can't rush love. The number of times I've found myself on a second date while simultaneously filling out our mortgage application. Take time to let things build.

In the words of Camilla, get to know someone before you start to 'like' them. Very wise words, young lady - it must be a Scottish thing. Thirdly, honesty. This one is crucial. You need to be open with your partner, as even if you think you are trying to be kind by hiding certain truths, these will eventually build up and cause problems down the line. And lads, don't forget, women find out EVERYTHING! Finally, if you do ever need some emergency relationship advice, don't forget to page Dr Marcel.

Over the past three series, *Love Island* has blossomed into a behemoth of light entertainment and that is down to the team. I'd like to thank them here. From the Runners to the Executive Producers, everyone went above and beyond to make this show the best it can be. The filming is next level, the production always runs like clockwork and every single detail, right down to the music, is given the utmost time and attention. This makes adding the voice-over one of the most enjoyable tasks I've ever been given. It is all down to you. So if you are a fellow *Love Island* employee flicking through this book, then well done you, well done indeed! You're the best.

Now that *Love Island* has drawn to a close for another year and my introduction is done, it's time for 'The Voice of Love Island' to down tools. So, until next time, be safe, kids - and be warned, if I ever catch you getting up to naughty business, I may just say something sarcastic!

x

Welcome to

love island ❤

ON PAPER

While you're reading this book, we want you to close your eyes (no, not really, that would be madness), but close your imaginary eyes and cast yourself back to the summer of 2017. A summer where, for the first time in living memory, the weather didn't matter one squiddly bit because, come rain or glorious sunshine, we were all indoors, sitting in front of the TV, doing the only thing that mattered: watching *Love Island*.

And boy did it matter. Miss an episode and life became one big spoiler alert; you became a social outcast, desperately trying to avoid human contact, praying you wouldn't overhear someone talking about who'd been dumped from the Island or who'd pied off who. If a conversation sprang up among friends (which, let's face it, it always did), you'd be forced to run from the room screaming, fingers in

ears, in case someone spilled the beans. The bottom line was, falling behind simply wasn't an option. Let's not exaggerate, but to not watch *Love Island* 2017 was to not exist!

But this book is so much more than just a nostalgia trip or a quick fumble down memory lane. Sure, there will be oodles of exclusive pictures and gossip from the nation's favourite all-inclusive holiday resort, but during the show our Islanders taught us so much about the noble art of grafting, cracking on and mugging off that we simply had to preserve it for future generations.

So think of this book as a manifesto for that magical L word: love. A do-it-yourself manual to building the perfect love life, if you will. The aim? To arm you with a bunch of invaluable tips and tricks inspired by our Islanders' seven-week amorous adventure. Follow this guide and we guarantee you'll be 'sticking it on' like a true Islander in no time, or your money back*.

Some might think that finding love in a one-bedroom, purpose-built shag palace, populated by randy, underdressed worldies, might be an easier ask than pulling some random in a supermarket or a nightclub, but the reality is, be it paradise or Poundland, the same rules apply.

OK, things moved somewhat faster in the villa than in the outside world but the feelings, flirting and fights were just as real. Indeed, the extreme emotionally charged environment served only to highlight some universal truths about love and relationships, and taught us some valuable lessons.

Lessons like - don't be backwards in coming forwards. How much time have you wasted in relationships playing guessing games about what the other one thinks? Not on *Love Island*. Our Islanders didn't hold back in any areas of love (expect Gabby, of course, bad luck Marcel). If they had something to say then they damn well said it, which made for some pretty awkward conversations for them and some pretty unforgettable TV for us.

For example, when Tyla told Jonny she'd had enough. Jonny may not have liked it (he didn't and we have the pictures to prove it! See Muggy Shots page 123), but at least he knew the score and was able to plough all his energies into brooding over Theo, who he nicknamed 'a gigantic bellend'. Another fine example of calling it as you see it.

Love Island also taught us that sometimes your type on paper isn't always the right person for you. A fact Olivia discovered during her dalliance with Muggy Mike. Although, to be honest, he's so good looking, who wouldn't take their chances? Most of all, we learned that in the quest for love

you might encounter muggy moments and you might encounter melty moments, but if you just crack on and keep grafting then you will eventually find love - or at the very least, lust. It's called the Sam School of Never Taking No For an Answer.

So, just for you, we've written down everything we've learned about villa life in this book, the official *Love Island* guide to grafting, cracking on, sticking it on, mugging off and finding love. So dig out your tightest white jeans, slap on your fake eyelashes, squeeze yourself into a bikini so small it's invisible to the naked eye and get grafting.

Whether you're a singleton or just fancy adding a little bit of Island magic to your relationship, then your brand new love life starts right here.

* This guarantee is totally made up and not worth the paper it's written on!

Love
Island
Essentials

#Life'sABeach

Love Island Essentials

#Life'sABeach

More than 60,000 hopefuls registered to be on *Love Island* 2017. That's four times as many as applied to Cambridge University, although we're not sure how many of those people applied to both. For the chosen few selected, it would be a holiday of a lifetime, where it wasn't just the food and drink that was all-inclusive but the eye candy, too!

On the surface of it our Islanders were off for a seven-week romantic jaunt to paradise, but in reality it was a trip into the unknown. Over the course of this chapter on 'Love Island Essentials' we'll be charting exactly who went with who, showing you around the villa, and equipping you with the vocabulary you'll need to avoid looking like a melt and get grafting like a true Islander.

We'd love to tell you that we really made our Islanders work while they were in the villa, but you saw the show! There was precious little work going on, but there was lots and lots of world-class grafting in an idyllic location rigged with multiple cameras and specifically designed to encourage maximum cracking on, which is what *Love Island* is essentially all about.

LESSONS in love #1   Have fun together

Relationships aren't always a barrel of laughs, so sometimes you've got to schedule in a bit of light relief. Some of the most fun we saw our Islanders have was when they were in the most compromising positions. No, not those positions, the ones where they had the entire contents of a butcher's shop stuffed in their bikinis. Sure, your fun dates may be more along the lines of mini-golf in the park, but anything that gets you active and joking around will do wonders. Planning some fun and spontaneous activities can remind you what you love most about each other while getting away from all the troubles of 'real life'. So stop arguing about whose turn it is to do the dishes and get yourself down to your local theme park. Things will look a lot brighter when you're about to plummet 20 feet to the ground.

How to Get the Villa Life

Pool, sun and sexy bodies were always the order of the day in the *Love Island* villa, but, as any true fan knows, you can never have too much information about your favourite telly show. So you know how they fought, flirted, grafted and got muggy, but how often did they change their sheets? That's still a mystery! Lucky for you, we've got the inside gossip. That's right, everything you need to know is right here, so you can make sure you are living every part of your life exactly like an Islander. You just need a few thousand pounds, dozens of high-tech cameras and a luxury villa. Easy!

Dress like an Islander

Being parted from your wardrobe for the entire summer could cause any normal person all kinds of problems, but our Islanders seemed to have an endless supply of styles at their disposal. Wanna know how? Well, firstly, the starting line-up were able to take a humongous suitcase full of 'essentials' into the villa, to make sure they spent the whole time looking their absolute best. Secondly, to make sure they never repeated an outfit, the Islanders played a game of pass the Prada (or Primark!). Basically, they all swapped clothes – it's not rocket science.

Eat like an Islander

Despite what it may have looked like, the Islanders didn't live off avocado and coffee in the villa. While they were in charge of their own breakfasts – made up of your basics: toast, porridge, eggs, coffee and avocado, of course – the rest of their meals were taken care of by one of Mallorca's finest chefs/the first one that came up on Google the week before filming started.

Be beautiful like an Islander

Being locked in a five-star villa for seven weeks does have its downsides – falling behind on your strict beauty regime, for one. To be fair, the Islanders did have a resident hairdresser in Kem, and the girls had no problem getting up close and personal with the wax, so the job was pretty much half done. Throw in a beautician who visited the villa midway through the series – true fact – and you're pretty much sorted. So there you go, get a few roommates who don't mind keeping you trim all over and, when in doubt, call in a professional.

Rise like an Islander

While some of the Islanders had VERY special ways of waking each other up, sometimes they were woken in the morning to the sound of their favourite tunes (turn to page 183 to get the playlist). So why not switch up your shrill drill for some *Love Island* bangers, starting with Blue classic – 'ALL RISE'!

Stay clean like an Islander

You may be wondering why, in seven weeks, you never saw one Islander change their bedsheets. That's because the lucky bunch had a weekly cleaner. Yes, she may have needed to be bribed to come back week after week, but, rest assured, the villa measured up to the highest standards of cleanliness. Well, kind of.

Stay safe like an Islander

Health and Safety is high priority for any Islander. Well, perhaps after grafting and cracking on. And looking good enough to eat... and eating... This is beside the point – safety is important and to prove it this year's villa was stocked up with 100 bottles of mosquito repellent, 230 bottles of sunscreen and a generous 200 condoms. Please note: These quantities should be adjusted depending on how many people live in your household and how horny they are.

FULL NAME:

Harley Judge

NICKNAME:

The Premature Withdrawer

Harley

Pre-Island Occupation:

Laying concrete floors (not a Judge, as the name suggests)

He's since moved on from floors to laying girls instead. Now, that is hard graft! #StayHumble

celebrity lookalike:

CHARLIE HUNNAM

Well, his sword might as well have been in the stone!

GETTING DUMPED

He got off to a strong start to the series when he bagged Amber in the first coupling and secured the first kiss in the villa, but Harley was left scrambling to hold on to a girl after bombshells Chris and Jonny rocked up. At least he still had his muscles.

fun fact

He once drank a glass of wee! But it was his own, so that makes it all right then...

6 days in the villa

Dumped on
Day 6

After losing Amber he tried to cut a very unromantic deal with Chloe to stay in the villa. She didn't go for it and he got the boot.

Amber

Day 1
Entered the villa

'I've got really good banter.'

celebrity crush:

He said Instagram favourite **ANA CHERÍ** would be his model girlfriend.

TYPE ON PAPER:

'A gym bunny with nice legs and a good bum.' Who cares about personality, anyway?

MEMORABLE MOMENT:

Ummm...

Hold on, he must have one... Didn't he do...? No, that was Chris... It will come to us eventually...

The Love Island Dictionary

As well as giving us plenty to talk about, *Love Island* also gave us lots of new ways to talk about it. It's no humble brag to say that our Islanders have taken the English language to a new level. This year they came up with so many new words it was hard to keep track, but fortunately for you we did. So now you can make sure you don't ruin your chances of *cracking on* with a *sort* because your *muggy banter* makes you look like a *melt* – just refer to this handy *Love Island* dictionary.

Scan this QR code on any smartphone QR scanner app to see Kem and Amber explain some of the Island terminology.

Aggy

Bantering

A

AGGY
adjective
Abbreviated word for 'agitated'. To be annoyed or irritated.
'Mate, I don't know why she is being aggy with me.'

B

BANTERING
verb
To say something in jest to evoke laughter or amusement.
'Are you bantering me?'

BARE
adjective
Slang word for 'lots of'. A term for much or many.
'There were bare girls in the club.'

BOVVERED
adjective
To be irritated by a particular person, topic or situation.
'He was pretending he wasn't bovvered by saying, "I'm not bovvered", but he was defo bovvered.'

C

CRACK ON
verb
To begin a romantic interaction with another person or persons with the intention of furthering your relationship.
'Mate, I'm going to crack on with Montana tonight.'

D

D**KSAND
noun
The trap of becoming besotted with a male or males around you and neglecting all other pursuits.
'I have fallen into the d**ksand.'

DUST
verb
Engage in sexual activity, specifically sexual intercourse.
'This is where you come to dust.'

E

EXTRA
adjective
Behaving in a manner that is considered extrovert, exceeding what is necessary for the current situation. Anything excessive and inappropriate.
'I can't believe they went on a date in a helicopter, that's so extra!'

Keep your basket open

G

GRAFT
verb
To put in a large amount of work to get the attention of someone you would like to be romantically involved with. Use flirtatious behaviour.
'If you want her, you will need to graft.'

I

ICK
noun
An emotion suggesting someone is no longer sexually attracted to their current partner.
'He's annoying me, I am getting the ick!'

K

KEEP YOUR BASKET OPEN
verb
To not commit fully to an interaction. Continuing to plot your course of action without an end goal. Weighing up all your options.
'If another girl comes in that I fancy, my basket is open.'

M

MELT
noun
1. A complete idiot. Someone that you do not want to associate yourself with.
   'That man is an absolute melt.'
2. Someone who is overly romantic and sensitive, or who is easily upset.
   'I can be a bit of a melt sometimes.'

O

ON PAPER
adjective
Referring to one's personal taste in theory, usually relating to someone's physical appearance. Not necessarily true in reality.
'He is 100 per cent my type on paper.'

P

PIE
verb
To ignore or reject someone who is pursuing a relationship with you.
'There's a reason why she's pied him off and that reason's obviously me.'

Graft

PUT ALL YOUR EGGS IN ONE BASKET

verb

To fully invest in one particular person or place. Mainly used in the negative, referring to keeping your options open.

'I like him but I'm not putting all my eggs in one basket.'

S

SALTY

adjective

To behave in a way that conveys anger or aggression.

'Why are you being so salty with me?'

SNAKEY

adjective

Behaving in a deceitful way.

'Theo is snakey going behind Jonny's back.'

SORT

noun

An individual who is physically desirable to you.

'That girl over there is a right sort.'

STICK IT ON

verb

To set upon another person with physically romantic intentions. To engage in touching or caressing of the lips.

'Tonight I am going to stick it on her.'

W

WORLDIE

noun

An individual with superior external beauty. To be considered world-class.

'Check out that worldie in the corner.'

Pie

Stick it on

Worldie

Which Islander Are You?

Some people spend hundreds of pounds having professional therapy and counselling in a quest to truly understand themselves, but why waste the money when you can do our reassuringly quick and refreshingly unscientific *Love Island* personality test instead?

Simply answer the questions below to find out which Islander you are most like?

If I was in a celebrity couple we would be...

A Posh and Becks.
B Mark Wright and Michelle Keegan.
C Donald Trump and North Korean supreme leader Kim Jong-un.
D Joe Swash and Stacey Solomon.

My favourite activities include...

A Discussing deep and meaningful subjects from sexism to the sexual prowess of your partner.
B Sunbathing and sex (not necessarily in that order).
C No time for hobbies, I'm too busy taking selfies.
D Grafting, cracking on and sticking it on.

For my birthday I want my partner to...

A Spell out their love for me in my favourite breakfast food. (Unless it's yogurt. That's just messy!)
B Take me to the Hideaway to do it like they do on the Discovery Channel.
C Remortgage their house to buy me a present.
D Whisper sweet nothings to me in an ancient Celtic language I don't understand.

If my partner said something I disagreed with I would...

A Cry and dump them.

B Have make-up sex as quickly as possible. (Actually, it doesn't have to be make-up sex. Just sex... with anybody who's up for it.)

C Hire a hitman to arrange for them to 'disappear'.

D Throw a massive strop, kiss the first person I could find and go back to my original partner with my tail between my legs.

It's important for my partner to...

A Be related to royalty, but failing that be more ripped than the Incredible Hulk's underpants.

B Be hornier than Hugh Hefner in a unicorn costume.

C Display totally unflinching loyalty to me all the time.

D Put up with occasionally being sidelined so I can spend quality time with my best mate.

mostly As

You are a classy, coy character, making you a definite Camilla type. You're one of those people who switch effortlessly from refined, 'butter wouldn't melt in her mouth' wallflower to seductive, 'Jamie stuck his tongue in my mouth' sexpot. You have high standards and insist on your other half being hotter than the inside of a McDonald's apple pie. Oh, and you cry at the drop of an aitch.

mostly Bs

You are a classic Mike type. It's like you and the Mahogany Sex Doll himself were separated at birth. Yes, you can be a bit of a mug on occasion, but it's nothing a good 'night' with a member of the opposite sex won't sort out. Embrace it. The future's bright, the future's muggy.

mostly Cs

You are an Olivia type, if ever there was one. You spend most of your life up to your neck in d**ksand and the rest of it fighting and 'f**kboy whispering'. Your relationship is so fiery, you need a bucket of water next to the bed.

mostly Ds

You are a born winner and a total Kem type. You're up for the banter and love spending time with your BFF, whatever your partner thinks. You have a bit of a temper but you find it hard to stay angry for long. You're loyal and bit like an overenthusiastic puppy, only with less butt sniffing.

FULL NAME:

Jessica
Shears

NICKNAME:

Shear
Glamour

Jess

Pre-Island Occupation:

Glamour model and social media influencer

Which roughly translates as, 'looks great in lingerie and is always on Instagram'.

celebrity lookalike:

She said
CLAIRE FORLANI

We said who? Jess is probably more famous than her now!

She can't feel her boobs so they often pop out of her clothes by surprise. It's all unintentional – she doesn't do it for the attention, guys, honestly!

KNOWN FOR:

HER (ALLEGED) EXTRA-CURRICULAR ACTIVITIES

Jess's biggest storyline took place outside the villa but it still had us gripped. Did she do the dirty with Muggy Mike while Dom was pining for her in the villa? He said no, she said no... We'll never know...

Dumped on
Day 17

17 days in the villa

Dom

Despite the slightly muggy way she got him, Jess remained with Dom throughout her whole time on the Island.

Day 1
Entered the villa

'My knickers will remain firmly on until I leave this villa!'

celebrity crush:
RYAN REYNOLDS

Ryan Reynolds was on a show called *Two Guys and a Girl* – sounds like a dramatization of Jess's love triangle with Dom and Mike.

TYPE ON PAPER:

Her ideal man would be '6ft 2in, have olive skin and dark hair'. Hmmmm... sounds familiar.

MEMORABLE MOMENT:

The Steal

As the Island's original bombshell, Jess wasted no time making friends. Instead, she decided to split up Dom and Montana before sleeping with Dom in the Hideaway, making them the first couple of the series to 'do it'.

The Couplings

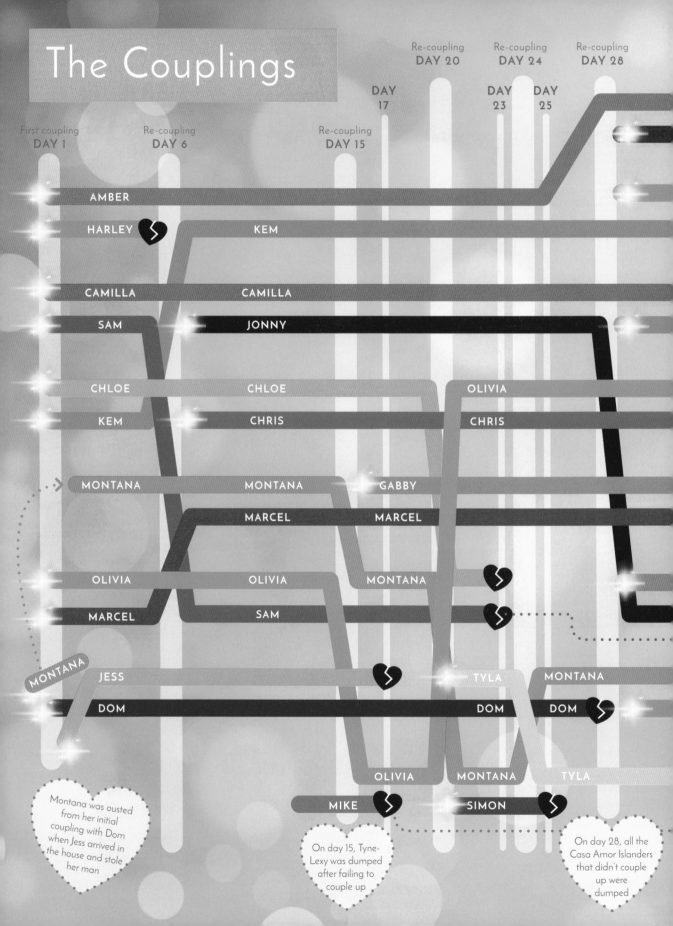

First coupling
DAY 1

Re-coupling
DAY 6

Re-coupling
DAY 15

DAY 17

Re-coupling
DAY 20

Re-coupling
DAY 24

DAY 23

DAY 25

Re-coupling
DAY 28

AMBER

HARLEY — KEM

CAMILLA — CAMILLA

SAM — JONNY

CHLOE — CHLOE — OLIVIA

KEM — CHRIS — CHRIS

MONTANA — MONTANA — GABBY

MARCEL — MARCEL

OLIVIA — OLIVIA — MONTANA

MARCEL — SAM

MONTANA

JESS — TYLA — MONTANA

DOM — DOM — DOM

OLIVIA — MONTANA — TYLA

MIKE — SIMON

Montana was ousted from her initial coupling with Dom when Jess arrived in the house and stole her man

On day 15, Tyne-Lexy was dumped after failing to couple up

On day 28, all the Casa Amor Islanders that didn't couple up were dumped

Re-coupling **DAY 34**   **DAY 38**   Re-coupling **DAY 41**   **DAY 44**   **DAY 46**   **DAY 49**

Winners

AMBER — AMBER — AMBER
NATHAN — JONNY — KEM

Second place

CHYNA — GEORGIA
KEM — KEM
CAMILLA — CAMILLA
CRAIG — JAMIE

Third place

Fourth place

DANIELLE
JONNY
GEORGIA
SAM

MONTANA
ALEX

Key

+ New Islander

💔 Dumped

TYLA
THEO — MIKE

Peacocking

#WorkIt

Peacocking

Introduction

#WorkIt

Our Islanders are a vain bunch. To be honest, it's amazing they stopped taking selfies for long enough to even notice their fellow Islanders, let alone go on any dates. But looking good is a huge part of the dating game, and turning heads and attention-grabbing are crucial components of the Islanders' tool kit.

The general Islander rule is: 'If you've got it, flaunt it, and if you haven't got it, get it and then flaunt it!' There is no getting around the fact that if you want to win in the world of modern dating then you need to really work it! That means looking the part as well as acting the part. So, in this chapter, we'll be giving you all the tips you need to get that ultimate Islander look you're after. Whether it's the micro-bikini-and-heels combo that's your thing or you're a fan of blood-stoppingly tight white jeans, this section will supply you with all the insider information you need to really make an entrance next time you hit the town.

So slap on the fake tan, get working on those abs and bung on an extra pair of lashes, because in the game of love it doesn't pay to hide your light under a bushel. Although, knowing our Islanders, they've probably all waxed theirs already.

Trust your instincts

Your instincts are there for a reason, so you have to learn to trust them. A lot of the time we choose to ignore the voice in our head that's screaming, 'don't do it', instead choosing to down another vodka and fall headfirst down the rabbit hole. A perfect example would be Liv, Mike and the d**ksand. Despite expressing to the villa that Mike was just like all the 'mistakes' she had made in the past, Liv still found herself hurtling towards him like a meteor ready to destroy Earth. Ignoring her basic instincts meant that she ended up stringing Chris along while giving off all kinds of mixed signals and making herself look a bit muggy. Even if the world is telling you that you should be with someone, only you really know how you feel. So stop making excuses and start trusting those instincts.

Get That Islander Body!

Being beach ready 24/7/365 is not easy and our Islanders have to work at it. When they were not grafting and gossiping, they were in the garden working out. Some of the boys were so committed to their exercise regimes that they even found time to do press-ups at night while they were in bed. Our Islanders' bodies are temples by day and fairgrounds by night, and it all takes a lot of effort. So, if you want to be a lean, mean, loving machine with a body like an Islander, get ready to feel the burn!

Alex's Abs

Alex is so fit and handsome that when he works out it's the people watching who get sweaty and breathless. We could show you how to achieve a rippling six-pack like Alex's, through a regime of endless sit-ups while looking in the mirror. But what's the point? You've got no chance. However, it's still possible to enjoy the washboard-stomach look without all the boring exercise bits.

TECHNIQUE:
Simply take an eyebrow pencil or biro and draw the six-pack of your choice on your belly. Hopefully, you will have cracked on before he/she notices it's an 'artist's impression'.

Tongue Aerobics

The tongue is the sole muscle in the body connected at just one end – true fact. And, like every other muscle, our Islanders like to keep their tongues toned and trim, even when they're not using them to snog the faces off each other. We saw plenty of tonsil tennis over the summer and if you want to make out like an Islander, what better way than with some tongue aerobics. It's time to get 'smooch ready'!

Gabby's Bendy Bod

Pretending to like yoga is the perfect way to impress a partner. If you're a guy, it makes you seem deeply in touch with your spiritual side; if you're a girl, it gives the impression you enjoy bending yourself into odd positions. Everyone's a winner. Namaste!

TECHNIQUE:

Essentially, just listen to the instructor and don't forget to breathe. If you're nervous of going to a class alone, you could try couples yoga like our Islanders did – although if your partner is as useless as Chris, you'll be more likely to leave wanting to drink spirits than get in touch with them.

Montana's Bum

So you want a bum like Montana's? Well, join the queue! Montana's bum was one of the biggest talking points of the series – everybody wanted one. Toned is an understatement. That thing could crack walnuts. The secret to a tight tush like Mon's? Squats. Lots and lots of horrible bum-busting squats.

TECHNIQUE:

Pull on the tiniest 'G-banger' you can find, so that your gluteus maximus is on full display, and proceed to bend your knees, pushing your butt to the ground. Do 1,000 reps of 200 five times a day and you'll have a bum like Montana's in no time.

TECHNIQUE:

Stick your tongue out as far as it will go, wiggle it around and try to touch your nose. Keep this up for five minutes a day for six months and you'll have a tongue like Harley's arm.

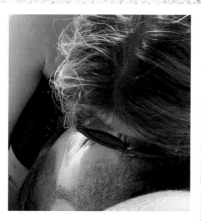

So there you have it. Follow these simple steps and we'll see you in the villa next year.

The Island Beauty Guide

There were many things our Islanders did well – partied, argued, lay by the pool – but there was one thing they did better than anyone, and that was look smoking hot! When you have a villa full of narcissists you are bound to run across a few decent beauty regimes, some of which we had never even heard of. So here is a little rundown of some of the Islanders' top beauty tips. Take note, and it could be you prancing around the villa next summer*.

Boys can wear nail varnish too

We're not talking about the black, 'fingers slammed in a car door' nails so loved by emos and goths. No, we're talking full-on glam. Now men can enhance their hands with a fresh pop of jazzy colour. Kem pioneered the 'male varnish' look when he donned some awesome pastel polish along with an even more awesome 'who gives a ****' attitude. It wasn't long before Kem's BFF Chris was joining in on the trend and we predict it will be the hot new look in 2018. Boys, it's time to nick your sister's nail polish and unlock a brand new you!

You may think you need to shell out £25 for a bikini wax, but think again. While Chloe and Montana may not have any beautician's skills, they were more than happy to give it a go on Amber with some wax strips and a towel. Now, you may end up ripping off a layer of skin too, but at least all your hair will be gone and you'll have saved yourself enough money for a round down the pub. Why not make it into a fun group night? Put that purse away and get your girlfriends round for a good, old-fashioned bikini-wax party!

You don't need a professional wax

Hide your spots with massive white splotches

It's a ballsy move on national TV, but sometimes when you feel the breakouts breaking out, you need to take action fast. Now we aren't 100 per cent sure what the mystery white markings are (some say Sudocrem, others say toothpaste and some people even said... actually, never mind), but we're sure we never saw a single blemish on Montana's flawless face. So we're off to hunt around the house for all of the above products to smother over our mush, in order to try and achieve Montana levels of super-smooth skin. Wish us luck.

A bit of spray goes a long way

Keeping yourself fresh includes every nook and cranny, as Camilla demonstrated when she started spraying her £100 perfume 'down there'. Now Camilla is the kind of girl who would rather give up tea and crumpets before she gave up her manners, so we're inclined to say that a quick downstairs spritz is something that should be included in any proper lady's beauty regime. If it's good enough for Camilla, it's good enough for us!

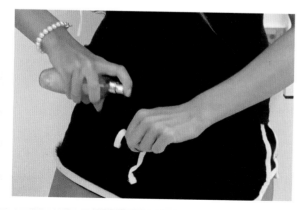

Deodorant isn't just for your armpits

While the rest of us have gone through life embarrassingly trying to wipe our sweaty upper lips with our sleeves, Liv has been living in the future and gave us an ingeniously simple solution. After you've finished sorting out your pits, give your upper lip a quick once-over with the roll-on and boom, your lip sweat is a thing of the past. You're welcome world!

* This book will not be held accountable if you do take note and aren't prancing around the villa next summer. Not our fault.

**Chloe
Crowhurst**

NICKNAME:

**Little Miss
Friendzone**

Chloe

Pre-Island
Occupation:

Posh PA

She was in charge of
muffins. Say no more...

celebrity lookalike:

THE
ENTIRE
CAST OF
TOWIE

The girl is like
a one-woman
Sugar Hut!

Sam

Dumped on
Day 23

23 days in the villa

Chris

Kem

Day 1
Entered the villa

Chloe once wet herself on a date. Well, it's one way to make a lasting impression. She also wet herself in a club – maybe she could start promoting adult diapers? #Spon

fun fact

celebrity crush:
DAVID BECKHAM

No harm in aiming high, love.

'Tall, tanned and muscly.' Such a shame there wasn't anyone that fitted that description for you in the villa, Chloe!

KNOWN FOR:

GOSSIP

Chloe was like the *Love Island* town crier. If there was ever a story that needed exaggerating, Chloe was your girl. She could make a visit to the Beach Hut sound more dramatic than an episode of *Game of Thrones*. That's why those lips are so big – they're literally bursting with secrets!

'Keep your pants in one bed mate!'

MEMORABLE MOMENT:

The Take-down of Mike

It may have been a tissue of lies, but who could forget Chloe's version of her conversation with Mike about Olivia? 'He called her a f***ing b***h!' Did he, though? For the record, he didn't.

Get the Look

A guide to dressing like an Islander

The suitcases might have been massive but the clothes were microscopic. The bikinis caused a shortage of dental floss right across Europe and when the boys wore anything at all, it was almost always exactly the same.

Now you, too, can dress like an Islander. Here, we've assembled some of our favourite outfits belonging to our foxy fashionistas and showcased during their time in the villa.

GABBY'S ENORMOUS EARRINGS

Despite the scorching 35°F summer weather, Gabby's earrings screamed Christmas-tree chic. Look at the size of those gold leaves! The poor girl will start walking with a stoop under the weight of them. We can't decide if Gabby's enormous adornments are more reminiscent of the bling worn by Pat Butcher in *Eastenders* or the chandeliers in the state dining room at Buckingham Palace. Take your pick.

MONTANA'S HOLEY SWIMSUIT

Montana is clever, beautiful and thoughtful. The girl would have all areas covered were it not for the massive hole in the middle of her swimsuit. What is going on? We think it might be the head hole and she's just put it on wrong. Either that or a giant moth is living in her wardrobe. Maybe in showing off her midriff she's trying to draw attention away from her perfectly formed derrière and giving everyone something else to gawp at?

GEORGIA'S RED DRESS

They say fashion is a statement to the world, an extension of a person's true personality. If that were true, Georgia would be a callous, man-eating *femme fatale*, and we all know she's actually really lovely. But 'that dress' made the wrong impression at the white party. For a start, it wasn't white, and secondly, it was a warning sign of the mayhem she was about to cause for Amber and Kem. After Georgia stole Kem from Amber's clutches, Amber was after blood – but at least the stains wouldn't show on that dress.

MONTANA'S MESH DRESS

From the swimsuit, opposite, it's clear Montana is not a girl who likes a lot of material in her clothing, and this eye-popping little number is barely there at all. It looks like it's made of mist, or perhaps some very finely woven net. If Amber's mermaid (see below) had got tangled up in Montana's net frock, we'd have had the makings of a terrible marine accident on our hands. Bottom line is, in that net-curtain number Montana looks like she's come as the front window of a nosy old lady.

The Girls

AMBER'S MERMAID DRESS

Amber's sequinned frock was something of a statement piece. Imagine if a mermaid entered *Strictly Come Dancing* and you're halfway there. Was she a siren luring men onto the rocks or a little package of fishy-fashioned fitness ready to lead them a merry dance?

THEO'S ANKLE SOCKS

'A gigantic bellend' Theo may well be, if Jonny is to be believed, but there's nothing gigantic about the rest of his wardrobe – check out these socks! Like the jeans, they're tiny. I wonder if he ordered them from the kids' section by mistake? Socks are never cool, but these would take the biscuit if Montana hadn't already eaten it. An epic fashion fail. Get some shoes on, they're hurting our eyes!

EVERYONE'S TIGHT WHITE JEANS

At the risk of sounding like the most boring grandad ever – those jeans are TOO TIGHT! Those boys will do themselves a mischief if they're not careful. But the tight, white ball-stranglers became the must-have look for the boys in the villa this season. Scientists and voice experts have estimated that all the boys' voices were at least an octave lower when they took them off. They also show that our boys were all individuals with minds of their own. Warning: When you are ready to remove these jeans after a hard day's wearing, please call your local fire brigade for assistance. You know what they say – no pain, no gain... Gulp!

A guide to dressing like an Islander

KEM'S SAILOR HAT

As well as being a symbol of his naughty nautical intent, Kem's hat reflected his playful personality. When he and Amber won the top prize, we're surprised Kem didn't start dancing the 'Sailor's Hornpipe'.

JAMIE'S UNDIES

The only bona fide fashion model of the lot and the one who needs the least clothing to look amazing! Why can't those pants be made from the same see-through material as Montana's dress? Calvin, if you're reading this, take note.

The Boys

ALL THAT GLITTERS...

Sometimes it was hard for our Islanders to accessorize their outfits, mostly because the accessories would have covered up more of their bodies than the actual clothes they had on. Luckily, we were able to get around that problem with a little bit of sparkle. As a reward for being average-to-poor parents in the baby challenge, our Islanders were able to get their shimmer on and cover themselves with more glitter than an Elton John stage show.

So any time you're worried that your outfit just doesn't have enough wow factor, take a leaf out of our Islanders' book and dip yourself in a giant pot of glue, swiftly followed by another pot of glitter. Just be warned, unlike with most things in life, putting it on is a lot more fun than getting it off. We had a sneaky peek through the Islanders' private photos on their phones to see who we thought had nailed the look.

Who ever said that glitter can't be manly? Chris went for more of an Eighties shoulder-pad look with his glitter. God forbid anything should get in the way of the world seeing those glorious abs! This is the perfect way to glitter up while still looking like an absolute boss.

The couple that glitters together, looks fitter together. Just like any good celebrity couple, Gabby and Marcel chose to coordinate their outfits and went for the same colour palette. All they need now is a red carpet. We especially love Marcel's glitter goatee – now that's a style we can see catching on.

It's as if Amber were already predicting her victory by creating her own glorious jewelled tiara. With her tiny bikini top, she was able to make the most of the giant gems on offer, bringing her outfit up from 'meh' to 'hell, yeah'. Too bad Sam's attempt at a glitter rainbow made him look more like he had been clawed by the world's most fabulous tiger.

Some people would argue that less is more, but it seems as though Montana in not one of those people. Sure, she looks as if she just grabbed a handful of the glittery stuff and started rubbing it on her chest like it were Vicks VapoRub, but at least her face sparkle is on point. We do love that Classy Camilla has perfectly coordinated her glitz with her ensemble. That girl knows how to accessorize!

Georgia was never one to shy away from a risky fashion choice, so it's no surprise she wasn't worried about the fact that she would eventually have to wash that glitter out of her hair. You know what they say, fashion is pain and she looks painfully delicious. While Liv's subtle face gems make her eyes pop, the chest pattern could definitely have used a little more work.

FULL NAME:

Dominic
Lever

NICKNAME:

Jess's
Boyfriend

Dom

**Pre-Island
Occupation:**

Careers advisor

Sod your exams, just work
on your press-ups and
go on a reality TV show.

celebrity lookalike:

He says
**BILLY
ZANE**

We think that's
a bit of a *Titanic*
stretch and say
actor Will Poulter.

Montana

Tyla

Dumped on
Day 23

Jess

After Jess was dumped from the Island, Dom refused to couple up with any other girl romantically, despite the rumours surrounding Jess and Mike.

28 days in the villa

Dom and Jess were the villa's original power couple

Day 1
Entered the villa

KNOWN FOR:

Sulking

At first, Dom was the life and soul of the villa. Girls wanted him and boys wanted to be him. But following rumours that Jess was getting mucky with Muggy Mike outside, Dom lost his mojo, his temper and, before long, his place in the villa. Dishy Dom became Down-in-the-Dumps Dom.

Phase 1: Get the kiss
Phase 2: Get naked
Phase 3: Hideaway!

fun fact

His real name is Anthony – Tony Lever! Yes, that's much better.

celebrity crush:
JENNIFER LAWRENCE

Yeah, he loves a girl who's down-to-earth and shuns the limelight. Right, Jess?

TYPE ON PAPER:
. . . .
'Great legs, great hair (ideally not on the legs), nice eyes and good morals.' I think Dom might be confusing the word 'morals' with the word 'boobs'.

MEMORABLE MOMENT:

The Reveal

It was the moment we had all been waiting for. The moment Marcel revealed to Dom the rumours that 'things went down' between Jess and Mike after they left the villa. There were bottles in the pool, a storm-out and… quiet acceptance and a return to sulking.

Butt Who?

After seven weeks of watching our boys strutting around stripped to the waist and the girls lounging about in bikinis so small they would barely show up on an ultrasound scan, we all got to know our Islanders' physical attributes pretty well. Butt – excuse the pun – can you recognize our Islanders from just their sweet little assets?

1

2

3

4

5

6

7

ANSWERS
1. AMBER 2. CAMILLA 3. GEORGIA 4. ALEX 5. MONTANA 6. AMBER 7. GABBY

Tatt Who?

There were some great tattoos on display in the villa this series. In fact, some of the Islanders had way more words written on their bodies than they've ever read. But can you identify the Islander from their ink?

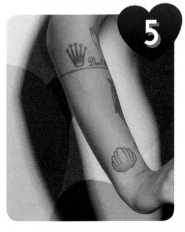

Kem's Hair Salon

style 1

With precious little hair on the rest of their bodies, our Islanders spent a lot of time making sure the stuff on their heads looked like they'd just stepped out of a salon, not a filthy communal bathroom rigged with hidden cameras. Good hair is all part of grabbing a potential partner's attention. It's also a tool for communicating with the people around you. A silent flick of the hair can say more than a blazing row when you scream obscenities and cry. But don't get us wrong, we're fans of both.

Hair maintenance was of crucial importance in the villa and luckily they had a hairdresser on hand 24/7 in the form of Kem. The glamorous stylist from Romford sure knew his way around a pair of scissors and, when you consider that his favourite pastime is looking in the mirror, being a hairdresser is the perfect profession for him. The big concern is who's he looking at while cutting your hair, you or himself? We only ask as we don't want anyone to lose an ear.

Before he'd really settled down with Amber, Kem opened his very own salon within the villa and, over time, cut pretty much everyone's hair on the Island. It was an ideal way of flirting, gossiping and getting to know his fellow Islanders. As a stylist, he's pretty good. At least, none of them came home with wonky fringes or dodgy partings. So, in honour of Kem and his magic scissors, here is a roundup of the best bad hair days from the series.

1. KEM - THE FIDGET SPINNER

Kem went a bit mad while he was separated from Amber and opted for a 'new hair, new Kem' approach to the crisis in their relationship. He looked like a fidget spinner but he didn't care, that was how he was feeling. It did mean that no girl would look at him twice and, as a barber, it was potentially a career-wrecking look. OK, have mini bunches if you're a member of a girl group or a cartoon character, but you're a hairdresser! It's not a look that instils confidence. Let's hope the rapping works out.

2. CHRIS - THE ICED GEM

The Iced Gem is the epitome of 'the do'. It's a work of art and requires intense maintenance using industrial quantities of hair gel. It might get it's name and look from one of the most uninspiring confectioneries ever invented, but it worked a treat on Liv and made it into her famous list of things she loved about Chris. We love it, too. A hairstyle that looks like party food? It's the future.

3. GABBY - THE PRINCESS LEIA

Gabby was never afraid to bust a kooky bikini or step out in a pair of funky earrings, so seeing her with her Princess Leia buns was no surprise and fitted perfectly with her bubbly personality. It was just a shame that the awesome new look came as she was having doubts about her relationship with Marcel. Gabs is clearly a girl who sees her hair as part of her emotional armour. Even though she was feeling down, the hair still had to be up!

4. NATHAN - THE FLAT TOP

Handsome as he is, how Nathan got on the show with a haircut like that in the first place is a mystery. Why Amber picked him in the re-coupling is even more baffling. It was a bad-hair day for Amber. Let's leave it at that.

5. AMBER - THE KEM

This is what you get if you go to Kem's salon and ask for the house special. This picture was clearly taken at a point when Amber was so in love with Kem, she actually wanted to be him. I hope they don't become one of those couples who are clones of each other, with a dog and a car that look exactly like them. Not a great look in our view - she looks very un-KEMpt. Sorry.

A Guide to Being Classy

by Lady Camilla Thurlow

Life in the villa was no picnic for Scotland's poshest singleton, Lady Camilla. She encountered some serious ups and downs during her grand tour of the Island, requiring her to show backbone, gumption and a Great British stiff upper lip. But through it all, thoroughbred Thurlow proved herself the classiest Camilla in public life. Forget that Parker Bowles woman (sorry, Your Royal Highness), our Camilla has grace, composure and looks way hotter in a bikini. If only there were a way that all of us could be more like her ladyship... Well, now there is, as we've assembled a handy five-step guide to help you obtain the same levels of class and sophistication as the one and only Camilla.

1. Get dumped with dignity

If your other half suddenly lost interest in your relationship and started charming the pants off a new flame in front of your face, you'd be well within your rights to storm out, get drunk and sleep with the first available human being, without even asking their name... Just us, then? Ahh.

But Lady Camilla faced just such humiliation when Jonny dropped her like a hot potato (probably a Jersey Royal) and started cracking on with Tyla. She cried her blue-blood-pumping little heart out to Gabby, and thought seriously about leaving the villa altogether, but Camilla is bred from sterner stuff. It was tough, but like the non-participating partner of pretty much anyone on *Strictly Come Dancing*, it's important to remain composed while your other half develops sexual chemistry with someone else on national TV.

Camilla did just that, and her breeding ensured she handled the crisis not through the traditional methods of binge drinking and casual sex, but with a rare and dignified stoicism not seen since the late Queen Mother visited the East End during the Blitz. When her man made a move on another girl in front of her, Camilla abided by the royal family's mantra, 'Never complain, never explain'. A noble thing to do, but ask yourself this: could you make such a sacrifice? Thought not.

2. Dumping in style

Camilla is one of those rare people who can walk with princes and paupers. She can snog them, as well – as she did with Craig, aka the 'D'You Know What I Mean?' bloke. What the literature-loving Lady C saw in him, no one could work out. Perhaps it was the fact that with no books in the villa, his endless tattoos provided much-needed reading matter. Nevertheless, it briefly looked like they could be the next Millie Mackintosh and Professor Green, but sadly, like the real thing, our short-lived celebrity couple bit the dust. Only this time, it was Millie, sorry, Camilla dishing out the dumping. Craig thought she was just being proud but it wasn't that, it was quite clear to everyone that she wasn't over Jonny. (That would take at least another day until Jamie arrived.) It might also have had something to do with Craig saying the phrase, 'D'you know what I mean?' a total of 42 times while he was in the villa. You see, she knew exactly what he meant and she thought it was utter codswallop.

In the end, although she dressed it up incredibly well, Camilla dispatched Craig with a high-end version of the classic, 'It's not you, it's me,' speech. Not an easy thing to do but sometimes you have to admit you have nothing – absolutely ZERO – in common and know when to end it. This was such a time.

3. Shhh! A lady doesn't kiss and tell

A true class act never spills the beans on a relationship, and sure enough Camilla was tight-lipped about her alleged fling with a certain prince before arriving at the villa. Admittedly, she was less coy when it came to the quality of Jamie's 'crown jewels'. Following a night of frisky fumblings with the hairy hunk, Camilla shared all the goss in the makeup room. 'He's got a perfect penis,' she confided to Montana and the millions of viewers watching at home. A crude thing to say, some might think, but in Camilla's hands even a penis becomes a thing of elegance and beauty.

I'm sure Jamie was pleased with the good notice. It must get boring always being complimented on his beautiful face and six-pack*. His penis getting all the attention must make a refreshing change. Remember, if you find yourself dating a class act like Camilla, don't show them your tackle unless you feel very confident of a good review.

*Many male readers will be envious of Calvin Klein model, Jamie. If so, try looking at it this way: Jamie is essentially just a high-end underpants' salesman – and they're not even his underpants! They're Calvin Klein's!

4. Intellect as an aphrodisiac

Willy talk aside, Camilla was also capable of a serious intellectual discussion. Whip-smart, with expert debating skills, the bomb-disposal bombshell raised the level of intelligent conversation in the villa. At times it was like watching Professor Stephen Hawking outwitting a group of seven-year-olds – oh, but what sport! Watching her school Jonny in feminist theory, or enjoying a robust tête-à-tête with Jamie about geoglobal politics, it's clear that brains play a large part of the chemistry for her. (I bet she knows loads about chemistry, too.) I guess the lesson here is, find someone with a similar intelligence to you, like Camilla did. After all, there's a reason why Stephen Fry isn't married to Joey Essex.

5. A swan on the surface

Camilla is like a beautiful swan. A picture of grace and elegance on the surface, yet we are never quite sure what is going on underneath. Camilla's classy conduct raised eyebrows when she made the shocking and controversial decision to do a workout in the garden wearing normal exercise clothes instead of a dental-floss bikini. Strange behaviour for someone who has chosen to appear on *Love Island*, you might think, but Camilla's hidden saucy side came to the fore while she was hosting the sex-positions game (told you she was classy) and she declared to the world that she was 'a lady in the street and a freak in the sheets'.

The phrase, it turns out, is an old family motto, which is currently being translated into Latin and turned into a coat of arms at a huge expense to the taxpayer. So remember, if you want to be a class act like Camilla, never judge a book by its cover.

Stay classy,

Camilla!

LESSONS *in love* #3   Seize the moment

As the kids say these days, YOLO! When life, or *Love Island*, hands you an opportunity on a sparkling golden platter, you take it. Learn from the mistakes of our two bombshells Marino and Rob (yes, they were actual Islanders!). Given the opportunity to get to know our six sexy *señoritas* (three of whom were single), they barely said a word - and, as a result, they got themselves booted straight out of the villa. Playing it cool can work wonders, but when there is a giant ticking clock over your head, time is of the essence. You can't always assume that the one you want will hang about forever, because the likelihood is that someone else will see exactly what you see, only they won't fanny about. Do you think Prince Charming would have just left Cinderella at the ball, then DM'd her at 3am? No, so get on your white horse, grab a glass slipper and seize the moment!

ultimate

JESS'S HAIR

TYNE-LEXY'S EYES

AMBER'S FACE

CHLOE'S BOOBS

GABBY'S ABS

I mean, the girl literally has 'ab' in the middle of her name!

MONTANA'S BUM

OLIVIA'S LEGS

They go on for days...

Islanders

KEM'S HAIR

MIKE'S EYES

ALEX'S FACE

As Montana said, Alex has a face 'carved by the angels,' and who are we to argue?

MARCEL'S TORSO

Can you believe Gabs gets those abs all to herself?

JAMIE'S PACKAGE

If it's good enough for Calvin Klein, it's good enough for us.

THEO'S LEGS

FULL NAME:
Jonathan Mitchell

NICKNAME:
The Feminist

Jonny

Pre-Island Occupation:

Business director

...of the family business that's owned by his dad.

celebrity lookalike:

WILL YOUNG

The boy-band quiff and wide, chiselled grin make Jonny the spitting image of the Pop Idol.

He once spent £1,500 on one date, but she did a runner while he was sleeping. Imagine his face when he realized.

Danielle

Camilla

Jonny and Camilla seemed like the perfect couple at first.

Jonny and Camilla spent 21 days coupled up

Amber

23 days in the villa

Dumped on
Day 38

Tyla

Jonny and Tyla never officially coupled up (thanks to a certain gigantic bellend).

Day 4
Entered the villa

KNOWN FOR:

BEING A RIGHT GRUMPY B***ARD

We all loved Jonny until his betrayal of the nation's sweetheart, Camilla, which sent him from happy hero to grumpy zero in record time. And with the arrival of Theo, his mood only got worse...

'I wasn't given a lot of choice because of a certain gigantic bellend!'

MEMORABLE
MOMENT:

His Bitch Face

It was the face that launched a thousand memes. The moment he chowed down on pistachios while watching his taller, more athletic and less grumpy nemesis, Theo, being cheered on by the whole villa. Poor lad... Right in the nuts!

celebrity crush:
ADRIANA LIMA

A Victoria's Secret model? Wonder what he sees in her then.

TYPE ON PAPER:

'Brunette, tanned, slim, small boobs, amazing arse.'

He probably should have added loyalty to that list... Right, Tyla?

Epic Island Fails

Our Islanders may have all been buff, bronzed and beautiful, but that doesn't mean they weren't immune to the odd complete fail here and there. Just remember, even if you're winning in the looks department, you still need to have your wits about you at all times - especially in the *Love Island* villa. But don't take our word for it, here are just a few of our favourite examples...

Stuck in you

A common fail - which you're likely to see outside any nightclub on a Saturday night - is when your stiletto heel decides it would rather get intimate with a crack in the pavement than help you get home to bed. It's annoying, yes, but at least there aren't 70 odd cameras around to film it. Step forward, Olivia.

After Jonny and Chris first entered the villa, Liv was so busy eyeing up the lads that she walked straight into - not d**ksand (for once) - DECKsand. Thankfully, Amber was on hand to yank her out of the embarrassing situation. Note to self: Keeping your eyes on the prize isn't always the best advice.

A slippery slope

Kem was no stranger to running up and down at the villa, but unfortunately he wasn't quite ready for the sharp turns of Casa Amor. During the Raunchy Races challenge, Kem's feet literally got away from him and he ended up taking a tumble in front of the entire villa. Unluckily for Kem, his fellow Islanders chose to use him as a human rug and simply trampled over him on their road to victory.

Rough and tumble

After spitting some bars in the Beach Hut, the boys learned a valuable lesson about working in a group. They were all sitting on the big Beach Hut chair when one of them stood up, throwing Chris off balance and causing him to take a dive. Luckily, they all saw the funny side and no one's hair was damaged during the incident. But how they expect to gain credibility in the rap world when they can't even sit down without falling over is beyond us.

Kiss kiss bang bang

He may have been your winner, but Kem makes it onto our fail list again with his hilarious head-bump in the night. Luckily, Amber had decided to freshen up when Kem thought he'd better check out the Hideaway bedsprings. In a fail for the ages, Kem's overexcited bounce resulted in a minor head injury, which even his sailor hat couldn't have protected him from. The lesson here is clear, kids: If you are about to embark on any overzealous bedroom activity, always wear protection.

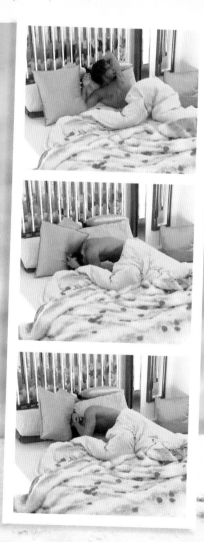

Grafting

#NoPainNoGain

Grafting

Introduction

#NoPainNoGain

No *Love Island* guide to modern love would be complete without a substantial amount of space given over to our Islanders' favourite pastime - grafting. Grafting, as we know, used to mean doing a hard day's physical labour, but the idea of any of our Islanders being capable of that kind of graft is, frankly, laughable. It obviously doesn't mean that any more!

Grafting, thanks to *Love Island*, now refers to the art of the chase, the wooing of the object of your desires. It's a crucial skill to master if you want an awesome love life like our Islanders, because, quite simply, no grafting means no sticking it on, which means it's only a matter of time before you get mugged off.

This chapter will equip you with all the techniques you'll need to get grafting like a true pro, from killer chat-up lines from our Islanders to a list of creative ways to say those three big little words - I love you. Once you've mastered the discipline of grafting, there really will be nothing stopping you pull the next worldie that walks by. Just remember, when it comes to grafting, you've got to be in it to win it - no pain, no gain!

LESSONS in love #4

Don't stick to your 'type on paper'

Yes, we all have a type of person that we are aesthetically attracted to, but does that mean that our ideal partner fits perfectly into that specific description? Absolutely not! While having a 'type' is inevitable, sticking to that 'type' is usually unattainable. Even if you were able to cook up your perfect match in a lab, including every characteristic you have ever been looking for, chances are you'd be incredibly underwhelmed with the final product. When Mike walked into the villa, there wasn't a girl in there who didn't seem to have his description neatly written down on her mythical piece of paper. But while they may have entertained the idea of a fling with Mr Muggy, no one was actually committed to the idea of becoming Mrs Muggy. Your 'type' may be a good place to start, but just because it's written on paper doesn't mean you can't turn the page and start again.

Grafting Dos and Don'ts

Sometimes it can take hours, other times you're at it for months. There may not be any set rules for grafting, but in the villa there were definitely a few lessons to be learned. Putting together a group of people who were more used to being grafted than having to do the grafting was like a scientific experiment. While some were able to pull it out of the bag, others needed to go back and try a new formula. Here's what we learned from our Islanders...

Do

Have Banter

Teasing someone playfully is a surefire way to start turning up the heat during the grafting period. Sam and Georgia went from mates to mating all through the power of banter. Whether he was asking her to make bulldog noises or telling the entire villa he thinks she should change her nose, there wasn't a minute that went by when these two jokers weren't trying to crack one another up. Laughing each other into bed is a strong start to any relationship.

Do

Play it cool

Even though she had spent a month waiting patiently for a man that she fancied to come into the villa, it didn't mean that Montana was going to jump on Alex the first chance she got. Montana sat back and let him come to her. And when he did, she made sure that he knew she was interested by... asking him to get the spider out of her drink (that's not a euphemism). It seemed to work, and in the end she had Alex doing 90 per cent of the grafting while she relaxed and enjoyed the ride.

Don't

Be invisible

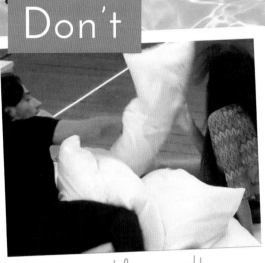

P*ss them off

A mountain of lies is not something you want to be keeping on top of early on in the grafting process. On Dom's first date with Jess he was honest

Do

Be honest

about his past (hours) with Montana, while also telling Montana that he was going to give Jess a chance. This allowed for him to keep grafting both without the fear of everything blowing up in his face. It seemed to make them both want him more, so there you go!

Always know where the line is! It's very easy to get swept up in the moment, but forcefully smashing a pillow into your graftee's face is almost guaranteed to cancel out all your previous hard work. It's important to know your audience, as Kem learned when he decided that instead of chatting with Amber, he'd start throwing the furnishings at her. Not only did she not take the action kindly, but he was left with his head in his hands muttering, 'I have f**ked it there!' An important rule of grafting: don't p*ss them off!

Don't

Be too honest

Before you ask, yes, there was an Islander called Steve and yes, he actually spent two days in the villa! While he didn't have any superpowers that we were aware of, he seemed to become the Invisible Man as soon as it was time for him to start grafting. There's playing it cool and there's literally disappearing before our eyes. Sure, you don't want her to think you're desperate, but unless you let the lady know that you're interested, you can't be surprised if she ends up with the guy who put in a good graft.

Oh, Harley... just stop talking! Telling a girl that if she doesn't choose you right then and there you are going to start grafting her mate is a little too full-on. Sadly, that's exactly what he told Chloe after sparks flew between her and Chris. Harley thought it best to explain honestly that if she chose to continue he would make a beeline for Camilla in order to secure his place in the villa. Unsurprisingly, this gossip spread through the villa like wildfire and resulted in his swift dumping from the Island. There is such a thing as being too honest, Harley!

The Snog Log

No audit of our Islanders' antics would be complete without a proper analysis of their snogging techniques. Our villa is the Wimbledon of tonsil tennis, the Wrestlemania of tongue wrestling – meaning what these guys don't know about kissing ain't worth knowing. So pucker up and get ready as we make our way through all the make-out advice we've picked up from the villa.

Sam and Montana
THE SURPRISE LUNGE

Sam was a lovely lad but he did go off like a coiled spring when he lunged, tongue first, like a frog after a fly, at an unsuspecting Montana. In his defence, for a snog to go well both parties have to really want it and truth was Montana wasn't feeling it. Sam got less lungey after getting it on with Georgia, but unfortunately he still has to carry the mantle of 'only reality star from the northeast who has never had sex on TV'.

Olivia and Chris
THE PENSIONER PECK

Despite spending every day lurching from picking fights to talking about what they fancy about each other, Liv and Chris did their fair share of snogging. If you can call it that. For two of the most attractive people ever to grow lips, they had a very questionable kissing technique reminiscent of the type of hard, cold peck your nan would smack on you against your will as a kid. Snogging is supposed to be fun and snogging someone as hot as Liv or Chris should be amazing. There is no doubt Liv and Chris really loved each other, so why did they always look like they were being forced to kiss their grandmas for pocket money? If snogging reminds you of going to visit an elderly relative, you are doing it wrong. It should not feel like you're necking your nan!

Alex and Montana

THE DON'T TALK JUST KISS

Alex was so quiet in the villa you would be forgiven for thinking there was something wrong with his mouth. Not so, as he proved when he gave girls across the nation goose bumps by revealing himself to be one of the smoothest snoggers *Love Island* has ever seen. Luckily for Montana, she was on the receiving end. The way he stuck it on her was almost as beautiful

as Alex himself. He displayed a flawless technique, cradling Montana's head gently in his hand as he put his previously underused lips and tongue to good use.

Chris and Kem

THE LITTLE BIT LEAVE IT

A kiss is just a kiss, but when it's with someone you love with all your heart it can take you to heaven and back. That was what we were expecting when, as part of the beer pong game, *Love Island*'s ultimate couple, Chris and Kem, were challenged to snog someone who was not their partner. It didn't take Kem long to reject all the girls and go for his bestie, but the ensuing smacker wasn't all it was cracked up to be. Yes there were closed eyes, yes there were tongues, but for some reason it just felt a tiny bit non-committal. Probably because they didn't want to make their other halves jealous.

Jonny and Tyla

THE WASHING MACHINE

Just moments after he'd kicked Camilla into touch Jonny set about snogging the face off Tyla. Actually, it wasn't so much a snog as a big open-mouthed lick. It was quite the production, complete with sucking and slobbering noises; the sort of kiss that startles horses and frightens children. Jonny's mouth was open so wide she could see his lunch, and what Tyla's 'pash rash' must have been like after stubbly Jonny's lip-locking, Lord only knows. Still, she went back for one last swim, sorry, smooch, just before he left, and that was a real spit-swiller, too. Remember, if you're kissing someone, they shouldn't need to towel themselves down after.

Olivia and Jess

THE I KISSED A GIRL (AND I LIKED IT)

So here's the proof that Liv can give a proper pash when she wants to! It was all part of a game that the Islanders were playing and Liv and Jess were more than happy to get tongues wagging, their own mainly. Poor Chris, settling for the pursed-lipped pecks of a grandma while Jess gets the sloppy Jonny treatment.

Whichever snogging style you choose to go for, always remember, never kiss and tell!

FULL NAME:
Theo
Campbell

NICKNAME:
The Gigantic
Bellend

Theo

**Pre-Island
Occupation:**

Professional athlete

Look out if you end up
sharing an Olympic
village with him!

celebrity lookalike:

WILL SMITH

Apart from being
one of the most
loved men on the
planet... Yeah, we
can see that.

He 'once slept with three girls in one day.' Hmm, considering your lack of success in the villa, I would be inclined to challenge that claim!

Despite his constant grafting and official coupling with Tyla, Theo was never able to win her over. In fact, she kind of hated him by the end.

KNOWN FOR:

STIRRING UP TROUBLE

He was the tornado we never saw coming. The mere mention of his name had Kem throwing pillows and the rest of the boys turning green with envy. Once in the villa, he insulted everyone, stirred up trouble and sat whispering 'mind games are too easy', like a James Bond villain.

Entered the villa
Day 32

9 days in the villa

Tyla

Dumped on
Day 41

'I think if Tyla really liked him she should go as well really.'

MEMORABLE MOMENT:

The Bellend Re-coupling

While the villa was still reeling from Georgia choosing Kem, Theo grabbed Tyla from right under Jonny's nose. After a few tense looks, Jonny stood up and called Theo a 'gigantic bellend' in front of the nation.

celebrity crush:
MEGAN FOX

Theo may need to do some serious 'Transforming' to impress her.

TYPE ON PAPER:

'Beautiful.' Umm, we might need a little bit more from you, Theo.

The Warning Signs

If our Islanders taught us anything, it's that grafting doesn't always lead to cracking on! Sometimes a perfectly placed graft can still leave you sitting alone on the breakup bench wondering where it all went wrong. Here are a few telltale signs to warn you when you're about to get pied off.

THE AWKWARD KISS

It's time to retreat when a girl looks like she'd rather jump headfirst into the fire pit than let your tongue enter her mouth. This was Sam's experience when he decided to lay a surprise snog on Montana after a chat about their 'spark'. If the reaction to your first real kiss is, 'F**king hell, I knew that was coming!' then you may want to get back on Tinder because this isn't going to end well.

THE ICK FACE

Sometimes they can be subtle, sometimes they're as obvious as a nip slip on the red carpet, but a guy's face can usually tell you everything you need to know about how he feels. There is no better example than when new girl, Georgia, revealed that she was tearing apart a newly reunited Kem and Amber by choosing to couple up with the cheeky Essex lad herself. Kem's face dropped faster than an unexpected Beyonce album, and it was clear that Team Gem was not meant to be. In hindsight, maybe picking a boy who had just asked another girl to be his girlfriend wasn't the wisest move Georgia could have made. Oh well, you live and learn, Georgia.

AMNESIA

Waiting two days for a text is one thing, but when a girl seems to forget your very existence, take it as a red flag! After 'twisting' from Kem to Nathan in the re-coupling, Amber seemed to twist back the second she set eyes on Kem with another woman, leaving Nathan outside in the cold (well, it was 30°F but you know what we mean!). While it takes time to get over an ex, when someone totally forgets that they have a present, it's a problem. If you're starting to feel invisible, it's time to disappear. Sadly for Nathan, just a few days later, that's exactly what he did.

THE SUBJECT CHANGE

When you sit down for a serious 'where is this going?' chat and your partner starts comparing himself to an Arctic animal, it's a bad sign! Chloe found this out the hard way as she tried to navigate her way around Chris's word maze. During a serious chat about their relationship Chris was more preoccupied with discovering his spirit animal (a polar bear, in case you forgot) than focusing on the conversation at hand. Chloe tried to call his bluff by asking him why he attributed himself to the most carnivorous of the bear species, but Chris replied, 'I don't know'. We all know making up wild animal comparisons with no rightful reason basically equates to saying: 'I'm not that into you.'

How You Doin'?

The Love Island guide to chat-up lines

Tyne-Lexy

Now, you may think that having rock-hard abs, perfect locks and a flawless face is all that you need to land the love of your life – and for the most part you would be right! But if you are one of those people who likes to add some actual verbal exchange to your usual mating ritual, then you could take inspiration from our Islanders' best chat-up lines.

'I don't like onion, but I'd do it for you'

Sadly, in the real world you can't rely on your prospective partner to be obligated to couple up with you every week, but you can rely on these chat-up lines to get you a little closer to your end goal. Some definitely carry more weight than the others but, just like a Domino's, it's all in the delivery!

WARNING: The effectiveness of these chat-up lines may well have something to do with the perfect human packaging from which they originated and, therefore, the use of them by actual, real human beings may be subject to dramatically different results.

If there was ever a phrase with zero potential to get a fella in your bed, it would be this one. Taking interest in someone is one thing, but when Tyne-Lexy sat Chris down for an interrogation fit for MI5, she may have taken things too far. Granted, you have to put in the effort to land your man, but chatting about vegetables is unlikely to produce results. It may provide you with one of your five-a-day, but you'll be getting nothing come night-time!

EFFECTIVENESS: GETTING NONE

Craig

'For me, you're every bit of my cup of tea!'

You may well question the rating of a chat-up line that likens a woman to the Queen's favourite beverage, but you can't ignore its effectiveness. Granted, Camilla was in a vulnerable place after being dumped by Jonny, but confident Craig's barrage of compliments won her round. There were many of Craig's chat-up lines to choose from, but his cuppa cracker was by far the favourite. One lump or two Camilla?

EFFECTIVENESS: GETTING CLOSE

Marcel

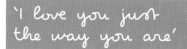

'I love you just the way you are'

When it came down to saying the right thing, there was no one better than Dr Marcel. The man could put out any fire with one icy cool line, so when it came down to reminding his girl, Gabby, that she didn't need to change to be beautiful, he summed it up in one swoon-worthy statement. Take note, fellas, flattery will get you everywhere (well, apart from where Marcel really wanted to go, but you get the idea).

EFFECTIVENESS: GET A ROOM

Mike

'It's a rare thing when I actually listen to a girl talk'

Misogyny at its highest, but it worked a charm in the villa. After coupling up with Tyla, Mike obviously decided that the grafting phase was over and it was time to get honest. Interestingly, the backhanded compliment left Tyla giggling like a schoolgirl before she stuck one on Mike's perfectly chiselled face. Worth a try, but prepare yourself for a rapid backfire!

EFFECTIVENESS: GETTING CLOSE

Chris

'Let me just grab it!'

There's being forward and there's being a bit of a douchebag, and Chris firmly crossed this line on his first night in the villa. After a quick drink with Montana in the Hideaway, he decided he knew her well enough to ask to grab her perfectly pert posterior (see page 33 to get the look). Judging by the Ice Queen's dirty look and Chris's failure to secure a second date with her, it's not a line to try at home.

Creative Ways to Say...

I love you

Skywriting, billboards, messages in the sand... These are all things our Islanders had absolutely no access to in the villa, so when it came time for them to express their feelings, they had to get creative. And when you want to outdo each other as much as this lot, you have to think outside the box.

Here are some of our Islanders' most inventive attempts to say, 'I love you'...

I love your unique style and the vibrant clothes you wear.

I love that when you kiss me you leave lipstick on my face.

I love that you forgive me when I make a stupid mistake.

I love it when you smile at me but do not say a word.

I love it that you're perfect, but you do not have a clue. I love that I can be the man to say I've fallen in love with you.

Jars aren't just for storing jam or for hipsters to drink out of, as Marcel demonstrated when he used one to store the contents of his massive heart. We all wiped away a collective tear as our resident hero showed Gabby how he felt in typical Marcel style. Luckily, unlike most people's experiences with jars, he didn't spend 30 minutes straining and struggling to get the lid off.

Jar of hearts

Write a list

Despite displaying all the emotional range of a fish finger, Liv did finally manage to tap into something vaguely resembling a sensitive side when she sat down and listed all the things she liked... ahem... loved about Chris. So if you ever find yourself stuck for a good reason why you love someone, then do as Liv did and come up with ten half-baked ideas instead. OK, so she may have compared his hair to an Iced Gem and his eyes to those of a husky dog, but for Liv that's practically a Shakespearean sonnet. And let's face it, nothing says 'I love you' better than reading from the Notes app on your mobile phone, trying to avoid annoying auto erections – sorry, corrections.

Say it when no one's looking

If your creative juices have done a runner, leaving you empty-handed, then why not take a leaf out of 'loudmouth' Alex's book and whisper it to your beloved while under the sheets, at night, when no one can see or hear you. Clever boy, Alex. He really knew how to get screen time, didn't he?

Use other people

Marcel might have been in Blazin' Squad, but there was no way Gabby was letting him into her knickers. So instead of using her body to show how she felt, Gabby drafted in the rest of the girls' bendy bodies to spell out 'I [heart] you' on the grass. It may have been dead romantic, but no amount of Vanish was going to get those grass stains out.

THE KEM INFINITY BRACELET

Now you, too, can be like Kem and display your commitment using one of these - an Official Kem Infinity Bracelet, just like the one he gave Amber before going off and snogging Chyna.

NEVER GET STUCK IN AN UNWANTED ENGAGEMENT OR MARRIAGE AGAIN!

Made from the finest quality synthetic shoelaces, the Kem Infinity Bracelet offers the opportunity for a unique, totally non-legally binding relationship commitment at the fraction of the cost or sacrifice of a real marriage. Plus, when you've had enough, you can simply throw it in the nearest bin. And you can't do that with an engagement ring, can you?

BUY ONE, GET ONE FREE!

An extra bracelet in your back pocket means you've always got a 'get out of jail free' card, in case you decide infinity is a bit of a big commitment.

Made with new and improved designer string, guaranteed to last into infinity and beyond. *

Infinity is not just forever, it's much longer than that.

* All guarantees are completely made up and not worth the paper they are written on.

FULL NAME:
Tyla Carr

NICKNAME:
The Cry Baby

Tyla

Pre-Island Occupation:

Model

We thought she might have been a tiler.

celebrity lookalike:

LUCY MECKLENBURGH

Carr & Mecklenburgh... They could open a law firm! Or, you know, just do some PAs together.

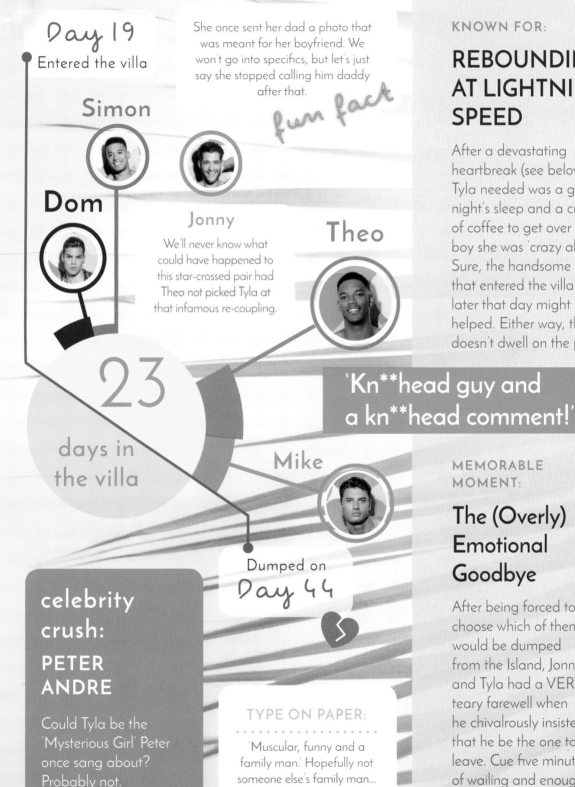

Day 19
Entered the villa

She once sent her dad a photo that was meant for her boyfriend. We won't go into specifics, but let's just say she stopped calling him daddy after that.

fun fact

Simon

Dom

Jonny

We'll never know what could have happened to this star-crossed pair had Theo not picked Tyla at that infamous re-coupling.

Theo

23
days in
the villa

Mike

Dumped on
Day 44

celebrity crush: PETER ANDRE

Could Tyla be the 'Mysterious Girl' Peter once sang about? Probably not.

TYPE ON PAPER:

'Muscular, funny and a family man.' Hopefully not someone else's family man...

KNOWN FOR:

REBOUNDING AT LIGHTNING SPEED

After a devastating heartbreak (see below), all Tyla needed was a good night's sleep and a cup of coffee to get over the boy she was 'crazy about'. Sure, the handsome hunk that entered the villa later that day might have helped. Either way, the girl doesn't dwell on the past!

'Kn**head guy and a kn**head comment!'

MEMORABLE MOMENT:

The (Overly) Emotional Goodbye

After being forced to choose which of them would be dumped from the Island, Jonny and Tyla had a VERY teary farewell when he chivalrously insisted that he be the one to leave. Cue five minutes of wailing and enough tears to fill the pool.

Casa Amor

The Neighbours from Hell!

Disputes between neighbours are common. Sometimes they're about overgrown bushes, sometimes they're about leaving the bins out and sometimes they're about trying to graft your neighbour's other half while they're not around. In week four neighbours were at war on *Love Island*, thanks to the introduction of Casa Amor. It was a huge moment in the series and almost saw future winners, Kem and Amber, torn apart for good. Here's all you need to know about the nightmare neighbours next door.

WHO WAS THERE?

Chris, Kem, Dom, Jonny and Marcel were first to enter Casa Amor on what they thought was a lads' holiday. They were soon proved wrong as they were joined by not one, not two but FIVE brand-new girls in the shape of Amelia, Chyna, Danielle, Ellisha-Jade and Shannen. But while the cat's away, the mice will play, and back in the main villa our girls were soon treated to some brand-new play things all of their own. Alex, Craig, Marino, Nathan, Rob and Steve strutted in with one thing on their mind... temptation.

HOW LONG WERE THEY THERE?

Weeks of hard graft in the main villa were nearly undone in just two days, thanks to the lethal, age-old combination of wine, women and carefully constructed challenges thrown in by the producers.

WHAT WENT DOWN...

Marcel snogged a shocked Shannen, not once but twice! It nearly caused a split between him and Gabby, and totally split the nation with the question: 'Was it really cheating?' Meanwhile, Kem was enjoying a passionate bedtime pash with Chyna.

On the other side of the fence, Montana met Alex for the first time and Camilla got to meet Craig, a man who was never sure people understood what he was saying, 'D'you know what I mean?'

casa amor

THAT POSTCARD!

In a world of text, email and social media, it's reassuring that a piece of old-fashioned snail mail can cause so much trouble. Wish you were here? Nope!

The Fallout:

- Gabby was fuming with Marcel
- Amber re-coupled with Nathan, a guy she'd barely spoken to
- Kem caused a ruckus by coupling up with Chyna, the youngest silver fox we know
- Montana coupled up with Alex, which meant it was time to say goodbye to Dom

What's Your Type?
ON PAPER

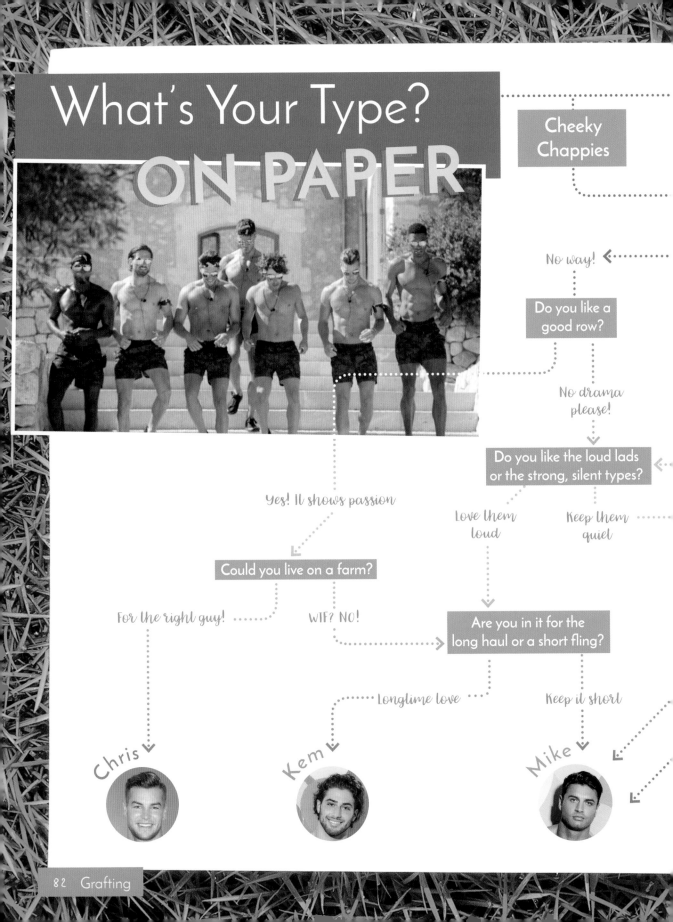

Cheeky Chappies

No way!

Do you like a good row?

No drama please!

Do you like the loud lads or the strong, silent types?

Love them loud

Keep them quiet

Yes! It shows passion

Could you live on a farm?

For the right guy!

WTF? NO!

Are you in it for the long haul or a short fling?

Longtime love

Keep it short

Chris

Kem

Mike

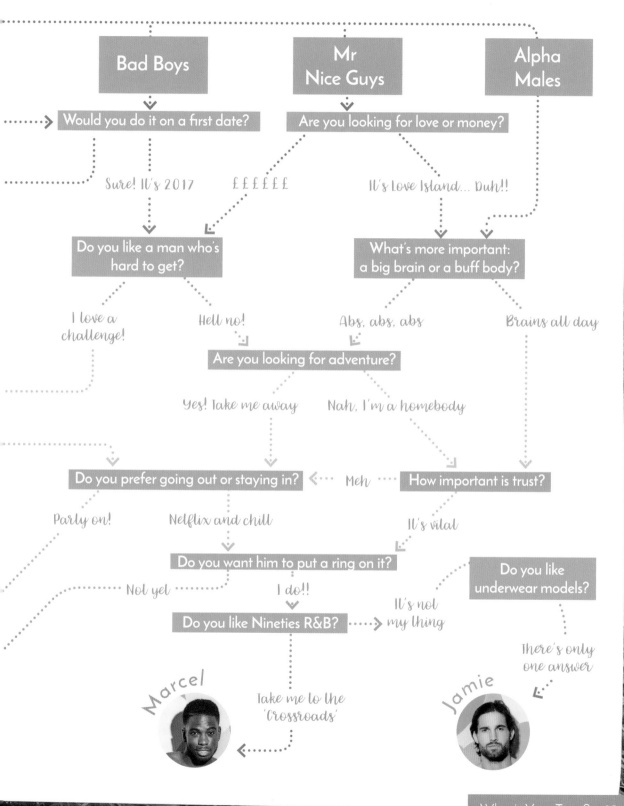

Bad Boys

Would you do it on a first date?

Sure! It's 2017

£ £ £ £ £

Mr Nice Guys

Are you looking for love or money?

It's Love Island... Duh!!

Alpha Males

Do you like a man who's hard to get?

What's more important: a big brain or a buff body?

I love a challenge!

Hell no!

Abs, abs, abs

Brains all day

Are you looking for adventure?

Yes! Take me away

Nah, I'm a homebody

Do you prefer going out or staying in?

Meh

How important is trust?

Party on!

Netflix and chill

It's vital

Do you want him to put a ring on it?

Not yet

I do!!

It's not my thing

Do you like underwear models?

Do you like Nineties R&B?

There's only one answer

Marcel

Take me to the 'Crossroads'

Jamie

What's Your Type?
ON PAPER

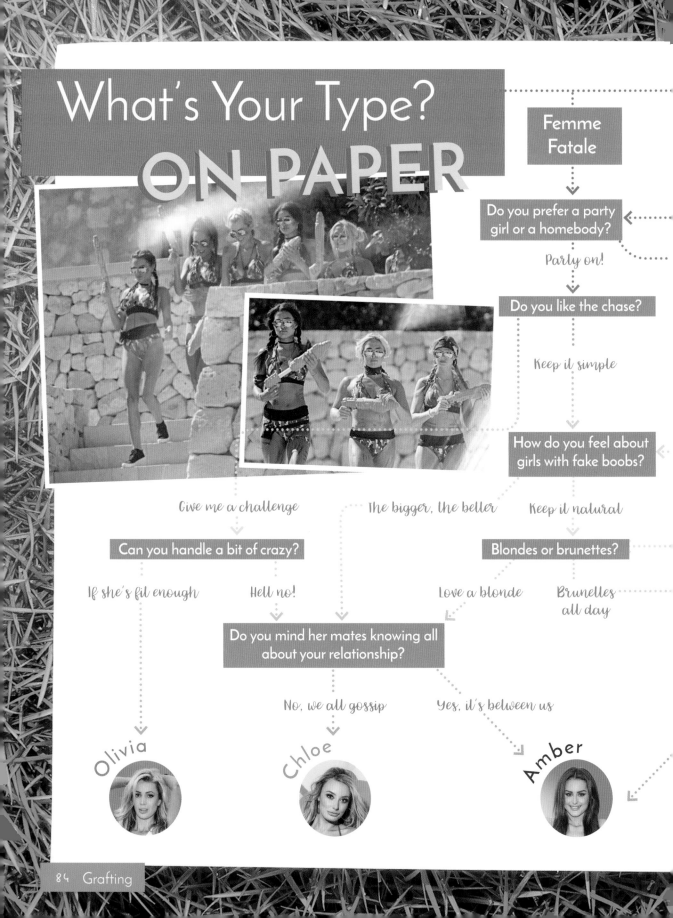

Femme Fatale

↓

Do you prefer a party girl or a homebody?

Party on!

↓

Do you like the chase?

Keep it simple

↓

How do you feel about girls with fake boobs?

Give me a challenge · *The bigger, the better* · *Keep it natural*

Can you handle a bit of crazy?

Blondes or brunettes?

If she's fit enough · *Hell no!* · *Love a blonde* · *Brunettes all day*

Do you mind her mates knowing all about your relationship?

No, we all gossip · *Yes, it's between us*

Olivia

Chloe

Amber

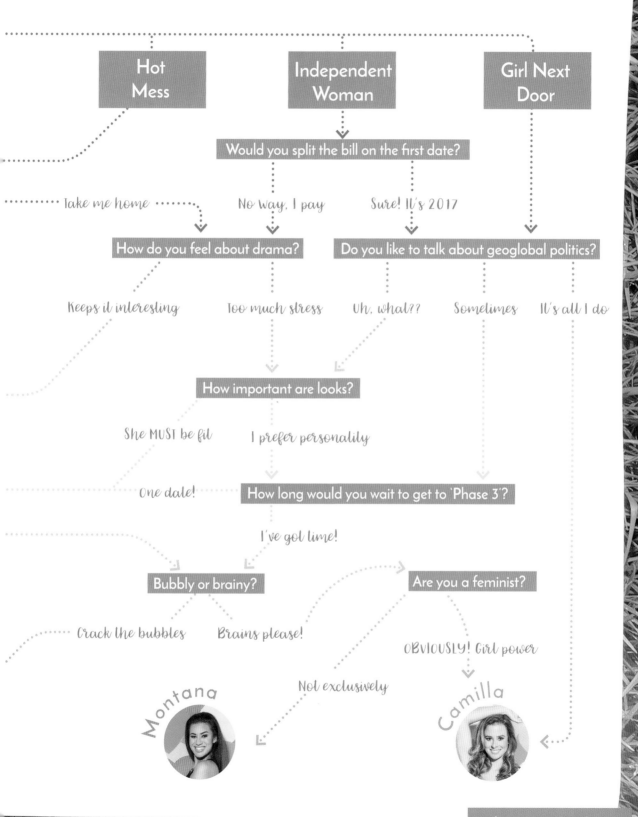

Hot
Mess

Independent
Woman

Girl Next
Door

Would you split the bill on the first date?

Take me home

No way, I pay

Sure! It's 2017

How do you feel about drama?

Do you like to talk about geoglobal politics?

Keeps it interesting

Too much stress

Uh, what??

Sometimes

It's all I do

How important are looks?

She MUST be fit

I prefer personality

One date!

How long would you wait to get to 'Phase 3'?

I've got time!

Bubbly or brainy?

Are you a feminist?

Crack the bubbles

Brains please!

OBVIOUSLY! Girl power

Not exclusively

Montana

Camilla

FULL NAME:

Michael
Thalassitis

NICKNAME:

Muggy Mike
aka
The D**ksand

Mike

Pre-Island Occupation:

Semi-professional
footballer

It was three years ago,
but don't take that away
from him.

celebrity lookalike:

CRISTIANO RONALDO

We'd say the
Greek god
Adonis... but that's
just us!

After originally being dumped from the Island after only five days, Muggy Mike managed to snake his way back into the villa, thanks to the power of the public vote. You wanted him back, and you got him!

Olivia

Re-entered the villa
Day 39

Dumped on
Day 17

10
days in the villa

Day 12
Entered the villa

Tyla

Re-dumped on
Day 34

celebrity crush:
JESSICA LOWNDES

I bet she wouldn't come to all your public appearances and stalk you, screaming your name and wearing a Muggy Mike T-shirt, though, would she? Not that I would. Errr, move on.

fun fact

He once nicked his mate's girlfriend and 'fondled' her on the bus home. Seems he has a history of muggy behaviour.

TYPE ON PAPER:
. . . .
'A natural-looking girl with a great sense of humour'. Preferably with a boyfriend!

KNOWN FOR:
BEING MUGGY

It was an off-the-cuff remark from Chris that branded the jewel-eyed hunk 'Muggy Mike' for the rest of his days! Whether he was stealing Liv, stealing Jess, stealing Tyla... Hmmm, maybe he should be called Mugger Mike? He inspired everything from T-shirts to... MUGS. And now, across the land he will forever be #MuggyMike.

'Did he just call me Muggy Mike?'

MEMORABLE MOMENT:
Return of The D**ksand

After he was cast out of the villa by his fellow Islanders, the public restored him to his rightful place, just in time for Liv to fall straight back into the D**ksand!

Cracking

On

#EyesOnThePrize

Cracking On

Introduction

#EyesOnThePrize

So the grafting has worked a treat and you've managed to win the interest of your heart's desire. It's now time for the exciting new relationship between grafter and graftee to really get complicated as things move on to the next level and you start mastering the potentially very rewarding art of cracking on.

This is where the romance rituals can really go up a notch. You've hooked your catch with your top bantz and awesome Islander style, and now you just have to reel them in. If ever there was a time for grand gestures and over-the-top public displays of affection, this is it. So in this section we will be arming you with our indispensable *Love Island* guide to seduction, as well as checking out everyone's favourite love nest – the Hideaway. So, pull the sheets over your head and start limbering up for some serious after-dark action. Donald Trump wrote *The Art of the Deal*; well, this is *The Art of Sealing the Deal: The Love Island Way*. They're quite similar, except this book contains longer words and better haircare tips.

Go for what you want

This is one that should be judged on a case-by-case basis. You can't just wait for things to come to you, you have to go out and get them. If we're talking about your next door neighbour's husband, it's maybe not the advice to follow, but if it's that hottie from marketing that you hang around the water cooler hoping to bump into, make the move! When Tyla entered the villa, much to the dismay of the nation she had Jonny in her sights. She made her feelings known to him and let the chips fall where they may. While Jonny had to let down a distraught Camilla, he proved that he wasn't the one for her, and then Jamie came along so it was win-win. Though Tyla and Jonny may not have lived happily ever after, she never has to sit at home on a Saturday night wondering, 'What if...?'

Island Guide to Seduction

Somehow, even when you put a group of hot, single sexpots into a shared bedroom, get them to walk around half-naked and kiss each other for sport, they still need a bit of help to get 'in the mood'. Luckily, the Islanders had the art of seduction down... well, maybe not down, but they tried their hardest. Forget wining and dining, this lot had to rely on their own special set of skills and we could all learn a thing or two from them.

BEGGING

Dom may have started off the series as the resident ladies' man, but he went from horndog to lapdog after his first date with Jess. After five days of laying on some thick charm, Dom decided to switch up his seduction tactics with some good old-fashioned begging. He may have sacrificed his dignity, but it landed him firmly in Phase One territory. Good lad.

LESSON LEARNED:
You're never too big to beg.

BODY LANGUAGE

Unlike her other half, Jess was a master of seduction. Simply squeezing herself into a skintight dress wasn't enough – she also knew how to work what her mama (and the wonderful doctors of Harley Street) gave her. From the sensual hair flick to a flirty bite of the lip, our girl was the queen of body-beautiful seduction. We are not worthy!

LESSON LEARNED:
A finger on the lip can lead to a week in the sack.

CONFUSE THEM

Sometimes a girl just has to take charge! After getting fed up waiting for Sam to make the move, Georgia decided the best way to seduce him was to confuse him. By getting him to close his eyes and cover his ears, he was quite literally defenceless against her charms.

A quick tip for readers: Make sure you are 100 per cent certain the other person likes you first, otherwise you may have a lawsuit on your hands.

LESSON LEARNED:
You can't beat the art of surprise.

USE WHAT YOU'VE GOT

She may have been in and out of the limelight faster than an *X Factor* winner, but in the brief screen time she managed to cling to, Danielle gave us a stellar crack at seduction. She may have ultimately failed to lure Kem to the dark side using the unstoppable power of her third nipple, but there was a brief moment when it looked like she had him. It was a risky manoeuvre, sure, but as any man will tell you a nip slip is a surefire way to get some male attention.

LESSON LEARNED:
Weird can be wonderful.

FLEX THOSE MUSCLES

Before he opened his mouth, Theo's seduction skills were working their charm on Tyla. To get a jump (quite literally) on his competition, Theo got Tyla's attention by displaying his athletic skills in leaping across the pool. In a house full of hotties, setting yourself apart is sure to fire up some passion – unless you continue to insult everyone, that is. Theo, are you listening?

LESSON LEARNED:
If you've got it, flaunt it.

SOMETIMES YOU'VE JUST GOT IT

So, Alex was able to get Montana to test out his bedsprings faster than you could say 'baby daddy', but it wasn't down to his romantic gestures or clever games – and God knows, it wasn't his chat! Sometimes you've just got the gift, and if you've got a face and body that have been carved by the angels, you don't need chat...

LESSON LEARNED:
If you look that good, don't talk. Right, Becks?

MAKE HIM WORK FOR IT

Sometimes you can seduce a man by playing the loooooong game. Gabby and Marcel were the most solid couple in the villa, but that didn't mean she was giving in to her basic urges. By refusing to let Marcel wrap himself around her body, Gabby had him wrapped around her finger instead, and she wasn't afraid to tease him with the occasional sexy dance move. They may have come fourth in the show, but Gabby got gold in the ancient art of seduction.

LESSON LEARNED:
Treat them mean, keep them keen.

FULL NAME:

Sam
Gowland

NICKNAME:

The
Comeback
Kid

Sam

Pre-Island Occupation:

Oil rig worker

You'd have thought he'd have been a bit slicker with the moves, then.

celebrity lookalike:

Former *X Factor* star
RAY QUINN

Especially since Ray's been working out - these two look like they've been separated at birth.

Chloe

Montana

Dumped on
Day 23

Seems like people couldn't live without Sam in the villa because he was voted back in just 16 days after leaving.

Re-entered the villa
Day 39

30
days in the villa

So many girls and so little romance!

Georgia

Re-dumped on
Day 46

Olivia

Day 1
Entered the villa

Camilla

celebrity crush:

EMILY RATAJKOWSKI

I wonder what it was about the 'Blurred Lines' star that caught Sam's eye.

fun fact

Sam used to be ranked the 102nd-best FIFA player in the world. Wow! It's a wonder he got onto *Love Island* with that kind of high profile!

TYPE ON PAPER:
. . . .
'Blonde or brunette, blue or brown eyes.' We're not sure Sam understood the point of this question.

KNOWN FOR:

STRIKING OUT

At first Sam had potential with some of the villa's most eligible bachelorettes, but one by one they all placed him in the friendzone. His reactions were even more embarrassing than his mass dumpings – 'I was gonna call time on things anyway.' Oh Sam, take it like a man!

'Let's see how much our love escalates. Is that a word, escalates?'

MEMORABLE MOMENT:

The Return

People may have been distracted by D**ksand Mike being back in the building, but the whole Island rejoiced as Sam burst through the villa doors and back into our lives. While we were treated to a sassier Sam the second time around, that entrance was a classic!

Re-create a Love Island Date

If your idea of a hot date is smashing back a couple of bottles of vino collapso at your local Wetherspoons before an argument in the chip shop over whether to stagger back to your place or theirs, then that might explain why you haven't yet bagged yourself a piece of Island-quality eye candy. Don't fret, because help is at hand. Here's all the info you need to re-create *Love Island*'s best-remembered rendezvous.

THE BASIC PICNIC

A picnic is always a surefire bet for a date, as Alex and Montana proved. A stone-cold classic of the genre, it's quick, easy and involves carrying a curious wicker suitcase full of snacks into the middle of nowhere before getting tipsy on a blanket. It certainly had the desired effect on Montana as she let down her guard, listened to her heart and agreed to make it official with Alex. He was lucky, though. Classy, romantic surroundings are all-important and Alex definitely took his eye off the ball on that front. I'm not sure what the sculpture in the background was trying to say, but I don't think it was that far away from what Alex was thinking.

If you're planning to give picnicking a try, be warned – check the weather! It's one thing pulling off a picnic in the glorious Spanish sunshine, but back home it's more of a gamble. Nothing kills the passion faster than a soggy sandwich in a bus stop during a downpour.

DATE RATE

GRAFT FACTOR: Low. A bottle of Aperol, some finger food and you're sorted. How hard can it be?

LOCATION: 2/10. Who arranges a picnic in a pornographic sculpture park?

IMPACT: Very successful. Montana said yes to being Alex's girlfriend. What more impact do you want?

ROMANCE LEVEL: 4/10. Despite the success of the date, the romantic mood was tainted by the location. A picnic in the shadow of a giant stone phallus? I think not.

ACHIEVABILITY: Easy. Alex achieved his mission of getting Montana to go out with him for the price of a baguette and a bottle of plonk.

THE LAY-BY LA LA LAND

Taking a woman to a secluded lay-by is hardly the most romantic idea for a date, but Jamie and Camilla managed to find a beautiful roadside location for their final rendezvous outside the villa. It was just like the movie *La La Land*, complete with 1950s Hollywood-inspired lamp post and a trio of professional string musicians. Although, if we're honest, it looks more like a training video about roadside rescue for the RAC.

DATE RATE
GRAFT FACTOR: High. A string trio is a definite sign you mean business.
LOCATION: 2/10. A remote pit stop is not the best choice for a romantic location. Good luck convincing anyone to come with you. You might want your date to get breathless but not because of carbon emissions.
IMPACT: Moderate. Jamie and Camilla were already pretty tight so this was more like a date night for an old married couple.
ROMANCE LEVEL: 9/10. If you put the roadside location to one side, then the rest of this date had a lot of horsepower. Re-creating a scene from a classic romantic film is a great start, but it was the attention to detail we loved. Remember the three Ds. Dinner? Check. Dancing? Check. Dress? This was the killer – a perfect copy of Emma Stone's bold canary number.
ACHIEVABILITY: High. A lay-by should be easy to find, and if you don't have access to a string trio then just ask your mate who plays a bit of guitar to come and blast out a few tunes, or there's always the option of a wind-up radio.

THE TOP GUN

In the final week Marcel and Gabby were given the A-list movie star treatment and sent out on a blockbuster dream date. A normal date might involve something like a night at the movies. But this date was more like being in one.

This is a tough one to pull off without access to some serious aviation hardware, so maybe just watch *Top Gun* on the telly while wearing massive headphones?

DATE RATE
GRAFT FACTOR: High. If this doesn't impress your date, nothing will.
LOCATION: 9/10. The sky! It doesn't get much better than that.
IMPACT: Successful. Marcel finally managed to get Gabby to sit on a chopper while cameras were rolling.
ROMANCE LEVEL: 8/10. Nothing says 'I love you' like a life-threatening grand gesture.
ACHIEVABILITY: Almost impossible. A seriously big-budget production required.

THE BLIND DATES

Jamie and Theo made a big impact on the villa before they even went in, by summoning a selection of girls to a series of blind dates. Nothing says romance more than lunch on a folding table in the middle of a garden of remembrance (well, that's what it looked like), and the girls were very keen to get to know the new guys.

Both Jamie and Theo were very relaxed. In fact, Theo was so relaxed that he didn't even bother doing his shirt up. He needed something to keep the girls' attention. Let's not be rude, but you could tell he was a sportsman from the dreadful quality of the banter. He made Andy Murray sound like Billy Connolly.

DATE RATE:

GRAFT FACTOR: High. Blind dates are all about making a good first impression. You have to turn on the charm fast, or just leave your shirt undone and hope for the best.

LOCATION: 6/10. Was it a topiary maze belonging to a country house or the grounds of crematorium? To be honest, we're not entirely sure.

IMPACT: High. Jamie and Theo managed to impress the girls and really wind up the boys. It was also where Jamie first met Camilla.

ROMANCE Level: 7/10. As blind dates go, it was pretty romantic and, as Amber admitted, there was 'good eye candy' on display. The banter was incredibly forced, though. You can see why these people end up sleeping with each other so quickly – they've literally got nothing to talk about.

ACHIEVABILITY: Easy. Like Theo, you don't even need to be able to do buttons. Although you will need to find a selection of hotties willing to meet you for a drink next to a mini garden hedge.

THE WET ONE

Not all of Alex and Montana's dates were as successful as the picnic (see page 98). Things were going well and he was lucky the tide didn't turn after this insane aquatic rendezvous. A crude raft of lashed-together driftwood is something you might put up with if you were dating Bear Grylls, but this was *Love Island*! Still, Mon had a good time, if only because they were given a huge steak meal with all the trimmings. She also left with a sense of achievement, having managed to drink red wine in rough seas in a white dress without spilling a drop. Result!

Pulling off a similar date with similar results could be a tough ask, but a can of lager in a rubber dingy on a nearby canal would be a good approximation and probably better than nothing.

DATE RATE

GRAFT FACTOR: High. When a date involves a sailing licence, you've gone all out.

LOCATION: 5/10. No one should have to try sailing a dinner table while out on the pull. Although the ocean is always an aphrodisiac.

IMPACT: Moderate. They enjoyed it but it was more of challenge than a chilled experience. Be sure to bring your sea legs.

ROMANCE LEVEL: 5/10. The aim of a date is to get the other person feeling lovesick not seasick.

ACHIEVABILITY: Hard. Any date that requires life jackets and informing the coast guard is probably going to involve a lot of work.

Written in the Stars

If, like the rest of the population, you've developed a huge crush on one or more of our Islanders, the best way to find out how much you really have in common is to look to the stars. Could you and Taurus Liv have the perfect bedroom chemistry? Is Aquarian Dom the one your charts say you should pursue? Keep reading to find out which Islanders you would be most compatible with in love - according to the highly reliable world of horoscopes. Hmmmm...

LEO (JULY 23-AUG. 22)

LIKE: Sam, Craig & Ellisha-Jade

Fearless, headstrong and extrovert, you have a strong influence on those around you, which is good as you are always right, or think you are, like classic Leo, Sam. On paper, you are best suited to fellow fire signs. You want someone whose middle name is adventure so Sagittarian Amber would be perfect - Amber 'Adventure' Davies to give her her full name.

IDEAL ISLANDER: Amber, Theo or Tyla

CANCER (JUNE 21-JULY 22)

LIKE: Camilla

Traditional, tender and loyal, Camilla is a perfect specimen of this crabby little star sign. Compassion is huge for you but you're also tough - there's nothing soft-shell about you Cancerian crabs. Ideally, you'd be shacked up with a Taurean, like Kem, except Amber would probably have something to say about it.

IDEAL ISLANDER: Kem, Jamie or Chloe

ARIES (MAR. 21-APR. 29)

LIKE: Not one of this year's Islanders!

Aries are creative, impatient and passionate and they like their lovers loud, proud and a little bit bossy. A Leo like Sam would be the obvious choice. Although his cocky approach didn't work when he tried to stick it on Montana. Probably because she's a virgin, sorry, Virgo.

IDEAL ISLANDER: Sam, Amelia or Danielle

TAURUS (APR. 20-MAY 20)

LIKE: Kem, Olivia & Danielle

Being an earth sign, like fellow Taurean, Kem, you desire emotional and financial security in order to achieve your full potential in both life and the bedroom. With his Sagittarian sweetheart, Amber, Kem achieved economic success - and we all know how he got on in the sack. He and Amber were the most prolific performers of the year.

IDEAL ISLANDER: Amber, Chyna or Shannen

GEMINI (MAY 21-JUNE 20)

LIKE: Jess & Steve

Kind, creative and funny, you're no stranger to emotional mood swings but can be a source of inspiration to those around you. Someone like Liv would be a good suitor, keeping you on your toes and laughing at your jokes. You're going to need a laugh - Saturn is rising in Uranus so expect trouble ahead.

IDEAL ISLANDER: Olivia, Sam or Montana

VIRGO (AUG. 23–SEPT. 22)

LIKE: Montana, Harley & Chyna

Virgos, like Harley, tend to be inquisitive, analytical and unafraid to speak their minds. Unfortunately, we've no idea if Harley has any of these traits as he was dumped before he could really get going. Virgos and Cancerians are supposed to have a lot of sexual chemistry, although the disaster that was Harley's attempt to crack on with Camilla suggests the stars might be talking out of their Uranus. That's two Uranus jokes now, get in!

IDEAL ISLANDER: Camilla, Jamie or Nathan

LIBRA (SEPT. 23–OCT. 22)

LIKE: No Islander this year!

Oh Librans, what a charming and stylish bunch you are. You love to be surrounded by beauty so the villa is a natural home. You're all about vanity, so any of our Islanders would be a perfect match as you're much too busy taking selfies to care.

IDEAL ISLANDER: Kem, Jess or Mike

SCORPIO (OCT. 23–NOV. 21)

LIKE: Alex & Amelia

Sometimes we wonder if Scorpios should be allowed to take part in the dating game – you're an unpredictable bunch! You suit partners with a deep, soulful approach, so Montana should satisfy your fussy side. You also have a sting in the tail, so someone with a wicked side, such as Mike or Liv, probably floats your boat, too.

IDEAL ISLANDER: Montana, Mike or Olivia

SAGITTARIUS (NOV. 22–DEC. 23)

LIKE: Amber, Chloe, Georgia & Marino

As shown by Amber, you Sagittarians are an impatient tribe. As dreamers, you've always got your head in the clouds, or under the bedsheets. With your sexual powers, you can basically have anyone you want. Take your pick! If it's your type on paper, it's yours, but Aquarians, like Dom, are your idea match.

IDEAL ISLANDER: Any of them!

PISCES (FEB. 19–MAR. 20)

LIKE: Jonny

You Pisceans are highly sensitive with a tendency to wallow in past mistakes. No time for that in the World of Love! Things move fast, so don't fall into the trap of being overcautious, let your passion off the leash. You like 'em mad and bad and in your bed!

IDEAL ISLANDER: Liv, Mike or Chloe

CAPRICORN (DEC. 22–JAN. 19)

LIKE: Marcel, Chris, Mike, Rob & Shannen

Capricorns have the patience of saints, as displayed by Marcel and his summer of celibacy waiting for Gabby. You are a thinker and an excellent judge of character. You probably used to be in Blazin' Squad.

IDEAL ISLANDER: Gabby, Steve or Tyne-Lexy

AQUARIUS (JAN. 20–FEB. 18)

LIKE: Dom, Gabby, Tyne-Lexy & Nathan

In theory, Aquarians like you and Dom are chilled-out artistic types, always on the lookout for ways to be a better person. If you can find yourself a Libran, you are likely to enjoy the best lovemaking of your life, but you are prone to making bad choices. Whatever you do, don't get emotionally embroiled with a Gemini... like Jess.

IDEAL ISLANDER: Kem, Craig or Camilla

The Hideaway Hall of Fame

Getting yourself into the *Love Island* villa is hard enough, but once you're in, it doesn't mean you have Access All Areas. Everyone knows that being in an exclusive club isn't good enough, you need to make it into the VIP area in order to be classed as a 'somebody'. Well, only a handful of our luscious lads and ladies were able to pull back the red velvet rope and make their way into the villa's most prestigious room. These couples may have already been established, but it was only when they made it into the Hideaway that they truly became a power couple. Let's remind ourselves of those lucky few Islanders who earned themselves an overnight visit to the villa's not-so-secret love nest.

DOM & JESS

The first couple of the series to break down the doors to our hallowed hall were Dom and Jess. On the night of Jess's 24th birthday, the Hideaway was open for one night only, and her fellow Islanders decided that she deserved a night outside of the shared bedroom. Shockingly, she decided to take Dom along with her and they ended her birthday with a bang.

GABBY & MARCEL

After asking nicely, Marcel was able to convince the *Love Island* powers that be to let him and Gabby spend a night away from the other Islanders in order to have some 'quality time'. Sadly, it didn't end up being just the two of them as they were assaulted by a particularly nosy and rather enormous bee. But don't worry, Marcel sorted it with a pink pillow. Apart from that, Marcel's grand plan led to more of the same – a lovely cuddle and a good night's sleep.

MONTANA & ALEX

The Hideaway wasn't all about the interior, it also boasted a lovely patio area where you could dine under the stars. While Alex may not have been the first boy Montana enjoyed a drink with out there (remember that date with Chris?), he was the only boy she decided was worthy of an overnight stay. It may have looked as though the genetically blessed pair enjoyed an evening of full-blown passion, but she assured the girls the next day that her Island chastity was still intact. Well, sort of!

KEM & AMBER

After getting the girls' hearts racing in the 'heart strips a beat' challenge, Kem won an all-expenses-paid stay at the local five-star resort, the Hideaway. Sure, he had to sort his own travel, but luckily he brought his trusty sailor hat along. They may have been the last couple to have stayed over, but they made sure our Hideaway got a very fond farewell when Kem got his anchors away.

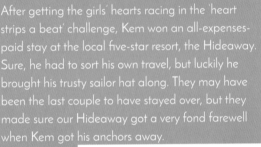

JAMIE & CAMILLA

It was another birthday present for one of our lucky Island queens. As if throwing Camilla a villa bash for her 28th birthday wasn't enough, her fellow Islanders offered her the gift of an overnight stay in the Hideaway with a certain tall, dark and handsome model – that's Jamie, BTW. As two people who loved to break the mould, instead of getting cosy in the Hideaway bed, they decided to enjoy the evening in the giant wicker basket outside. They didn't go all the way on that romantic evening, but decided to wait until they were back sharing a room with ten other people instead.

FULL NAME:

Georgia
Harrison

NICKNAME:

The Red
Rebel

Georgia

**Pre-Island
Occupation:**

PA to a CEO

She says she
was her boss's
favourite. I bet his
wife loved that!

celebrity lookalike:

TILLY KEEPER

With their long blonde
locks and petite frames,
Georgia and Louise
Mitchell in *Eastenders*
could be twins.

Her ex once threw a glass of red wine over her because she was screaming at him so loudly. I mean, that's one way to shut someone up. Red wine, though... at least go for the white - so much easier to get out.

Entered the villa
Day 34

12
days in the villa

Kem (awks)

Day 46
Dumped

Sam

KNOWN FOR:

PLAYING A DANGEROUS GAME

From the moment she strutted into the white party in a red dress, Georgia made it clear she would ruffle feathers. Whether she was flirting with the boys or upsetting the girls, she was ripping up the rule book and playing the dangerous game. You go girl!

'I don't feel the need to play it safe.'

celebrity crush:
JUSTIN BIEBER

Well, she did say she likes a 'Baby' face, so I bet she'd love him to be her 'Boyfriend', but she wouldn't act 'Despacito'... Not sure what that means, but you get where we're going with this.

Georgia's coupling with Kem was short-lived, but luckily with the return of Sam to the villa she was able to find love, or at least some mild lust. Sadly, the pair's quick-fire romance wasn't able to compete with the long-term loves of the villa, and they were soon dumped from the Island.

TYPE ON PAPER:
· · · · · · · · · · · · · · · · · · · ·
'A boy with a baby-face who's confident and cocky.' Hello Sam! I mean, that's pretty much dead on. *Love Island* strikes again!

MEMORABLE MOMENT:

Stealing Kem

The gasps could be heard in Casa Amor... OK, that's not far, but they were only gasps! When Georgia put a stop to the long-awaited reunion of our eventual winners, Kem and Amber, it knocked the villa sideways and kicked off the most dramatic re-coupling in *Love Island* history.

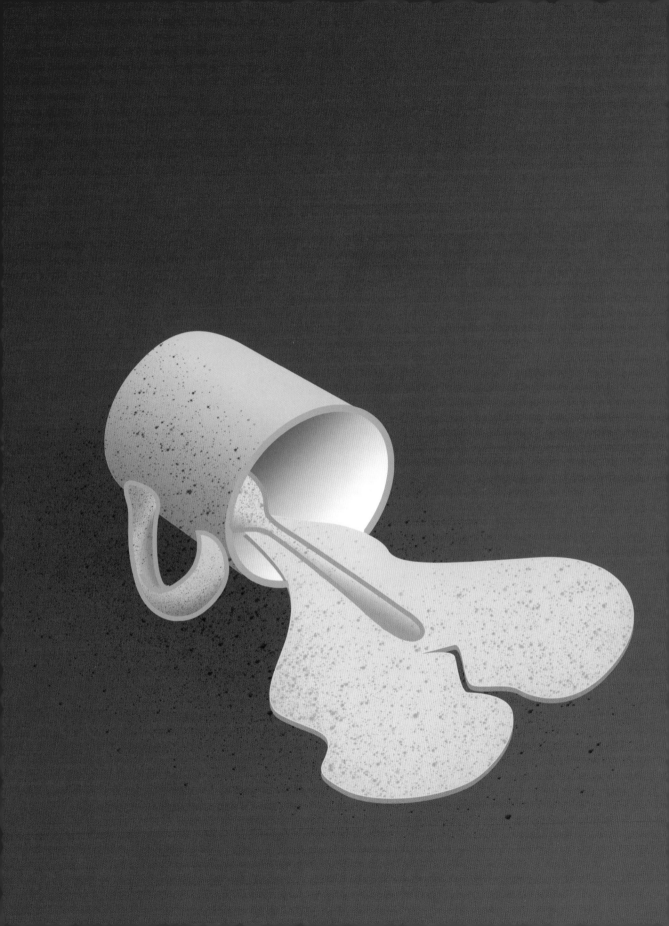

Mugging Off

Off

#MugLife

Mugging Off

#MugLife

To be a mug in the *Love Island* villa is about the worst thing it's possible to be. Yet pretty much everyone has had a muggy moment at some time or another – not just poor old Muggy Mike, who got lumbered with the nickname early doors and is now stuck with it for all eternity.

Mugging off your other half can involve anything from throwing shade, to throwing a tantrum, to throwing all your worldly possessions out of the bedroom window. OK, that's going a bit far but you get the idea.

In this section we will be checking out the villa's most vicious bust-ups as well as some of our Islanders' most muggy moments. It's an important area of Island life and a reminder that the journey to love is never plain sailing. But why focus on the negatives, I hear you ask? Well, firstly, it's important to try to learn from our Islanders' mistakes so as not to repeat them in our own love lives. But also, be honest, who doesn't enjoy being reminded of our Islanders' most awkward and embarrassing moments? So just relax – and remember, it's funny because it isn't you.

LESSONS in love #6 Don't force it

This lesson applies in many other walks of life as well, but today let's focus it on love. While you may be on a mission to get over the one that got away, it doesn't mean you should shack up with the first little hottie that takes your fancy. During his time in Casa Amor, Kem convinced himself that getting under someone else would get him over Amber, and look how that turned out. Not only did he end up hurting Amber with that poisoned postcard, but he also caught Chyna in the crossfire. Taking your mind off your breakup is always a good step, but you can't put a bandage on a broken heart. If Kem had taken the time to figure out what he wanted, he wouldn't have had a villa of angry girls to deal with on his return.

Mugging Off Dos and Don'ts

Let's face it, mugging someone off or being mugged off is never easy, but sometimes in life cutting the relationship cord is a necessity. Whether your relationship has reached its end or someone is beginning to get on your last nerve, there is no hiding from the inevitable. By studying the Islanders' mugging off successes and failures, we've compiled a handy guide to help you get your master's in mugging.

Do

Talk to your friends about it

The first thing you need to do when you've been mugged off is call the squad round, uncork the wine and get it all out. Talking it through with your nearest and dearest goes a long way to getting over a breakup, and is a lot cheaper than therapy. It can help you to make sense of the situation while allowing your mates to remind you just how amazing you are.

Do

Have the tough talk

It's awkward, it's uncomfortable, but it's got to be done. An 'It's not you, it's me' text may be convenient but it's guaranteed to land you in f**kboy territory. It may have taken some time, but Jonny finally sat Camilla down and told her it wasn't working.

While he got the first phase of mugging off sorted, Jonny quickly forgot all his gentlemanly manners and started thinking with his... little Jonny! The same night he cooled things with Camilla, he started tonguing Tyla right next to her. You are entitled to move on, but maybe try waiting a casual few days before you start copping off with someone else.

Don't

Kiss another girl five minutes later

Don't

Immediately start bitching

It's natural to be angry, but heading straight over to your mutual friends to tell them what a d**k your ex-fella is definitely makes you look like the bitter ex. While Chloe may not have been thrilled that Chris dumped her in order to crack on with one of her mates, bad-mouthing him around the fire pit did her no favours and caused even bigger problems. Keep a cool head and you'll look like the classiest girl around... Right, Camilla?

When it comes to being mugged off, there is no better example of how to take it like a champ. Montana listened to Dom's reasons but made sure he knew exactly what she thought about the situation, without getting angry. Just because you're being mugged off doesn't mean you should be treated like a mug! Make sure that you get everything off your chest and then you can walk away with no ties.

Do

Explain your feelings

Don't

Say you're not bovvered

He did many things well but being mugged off was not one of them. Poor Chris could never quite get over Liv's attraction to the muggiest of all men, Mike, choosing instead to repeatedly tell Liv that he was 'not bovvered' by the situation. Not only did this make him come across extremely 'bovvered', but it also pushed Liv straight into the arms of another man. It's OK to be 'bovvered' – maybe just don't keep repeating the term, or at least pronounce it correctly.

FULL NAME:
Montana
Brown

NICKNAME:
Ice Queen

Montana

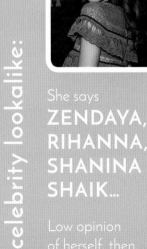

**Pre-Island
Occupation:**

Economics student

Well, she did know a lot
of big words.

celebrity lookalike:

She says
**ZENDAYA,
RIHANNA,
SHANINA
SHAIK...**

Low opinion
of herself, then.

Simon

Dom

Sam

Marcel

Montana and Alex JUST missed out on the final

50 days in the villa

Alex

One positive thing to come out of the Casa Amor split was Montana finally finding her man in Alex.

Day 1
Entered the villa

Day 50
Dumped

KNOWN FOR:

EATING

Whether she was surrounded by breakups, breakdowns or people breaking furniture, you could always count on our girl to be chowing down.

'Found the baby daddy!'

celebrity crush:
'LOCKIE' FROM TOWIE

Aim low and you'll never be disappointed!

fun fact

Before she went into the villa her family thought she was a virgin. Don't worry, Mon, they'll never guess.

TYPE ON PAPER:

'Over 6ft 1in, muscly, good teeth, blonde and no slip-on brown shoes.' Not fussy then, Mon?

MEMORABLE MOMENT:

The Morning After

Roughly 0.7 seconds after leaving the Hideaway with Alex, Mon was surrounded by her squad for a dirty debrief.

Montana 115

How Muggy Are You?

A Mug's Checklist

Let's face it, nobody's perfect, occasionally we can all be a bit muggy. But just how big a mug are you? Are you merely espresso sized or more like one of those giant Sports Direct mugs? Well, wonder no more. Here's a handy checklist to measure your mugginess against everyone's favourite mug – Muggy Mike!

Have you ever...

- ☐ Dumped someone via text
- ☐ Made fun of someone behind their back
- ☐ Gone through someone's phone
- ☐ Kissed two people in one night
- ☐ Stood someone up on a date
- ☐ Left a date halfway through
- ☐ Made your date pay for the entire night
- ☐ Thought about someone else during sex
- ☐ Ignored a text from someone you're dating
- ☐ Ghosted someone you're dating
- ☐ Meddled in someone else's relationship
- ☐ Kissed a friend of your ex
- ☐ Told a lie to get someone into bed
- ☐ Flirted with someone else's partner
- ☐ Dated someone else's partner
- ☐ Kissed someone else's partner
- ☐ Had sex with someone else's partner
- ☐ Lied about being single
- ☐ Kicked someone out the next morning
- ☐ Pretended to like someone you didn't
- ☐ Spread a rumour about a friend
- ☐ Kissed a friend's boyfriend/girlfriend
- ☐ Slept with a friend's boyfriend/girlfriend
- ☐ Cheated on your partner
- ☐ Sexted someone behind your partner's back
- ☐ Double-dipped
- ☐ Used sex to get what you want
- ☐ Lied to your partner about where you were
- ☐ Got with a mate's sibling
- ☐ Got with a mate's parent

MUGGY MIKE

You are as muggy as the man himself! You see a muggy situation and run straight towards it to see how you can make it worse. You get muggier with each passing second and you can't wait to see who you'll mug off next. It's gonna be a muggy life for you, my friend. #StayMuggy

You Scored 20+

MEDIUM-STYLE MUGGY

You know what's wrong but sometimes you just want to be bad! It's a muggy slope that you are consciously sliding down. While you don't do it to be malicious, being muggy is something you enjoy from time to time. But beware, it's a short leap from medium muggy to full-blown Mike!

You Scored 10-20

A MEEK MUG

Sure, you've got some muggy traits but you're an all-round decent human being. While you can be tempted by some of the muggier things in life, you tend to try and avoid them. Stay on that path and you'll shake that muggy off in no time.

You Scored 1-10

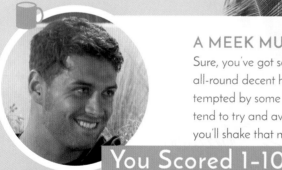

It's a Bust... Up!

While the show may have been called *Love Island*, it wouldn't have been half as entertaining if there hadn't been a bit of tension thrown in. Who would have thought that people fighting to find love would still have the remaining energy to fight among themselves? Well, somehow they managed it, and there were a few villa bust-ups that are definitely worth a mention. Interestingly, we seem to have unearthed a pattern when it comes to a *Love Island* argument; one bust-up seemed to set off a chain of events. Take a look...

CAMILLA

After a clash about the true meaning of feminism (yep, *Love Island* does politics... sometimes!), the pair exchanged some heated words in which Jonny called Cam 'bitchy' and Camilla, well, she cried a lot.

JONNY

After being the subject of Camilla's displeasure, it was time for Jonny to find someone to take his anger out on, and that person came in the 6ft 5in package of Theo. After trying to crack on with Jonny's girl, Theo found himself tasting his wrath.

THEO

Following the 'bellend' re-coupling, it was time for Theo to let out some built-up aggression, and this time the target was Tyla. Talk about kicking someone when they're down – Theo decided to pick a fight with Tyla during her emotional farewell with Jonny. While she gave as good as she got, luckily Tyla chose not to pay it forward, so the bust-ups chain ended there.

SAM

Sam thought he had a good thing going with Liv, until fit farm boy, Chris, walked onto the scene. After deciding to clear the air, all hell broke loose as Sam tried to warn Chris off his girl. Thankfully, the rest of the boys were able to break up the fight before any real damage was done.

CHRIS

Not long after Sam had unleashed a tirade of anger onto him, Chris took aim at Amber after she twisted his words and made Kem believe that he was cracking on to her. Chris was not backing down on the issue, and firmly let Amber know where she stood.

AMBER

So, it seems karma came back to bite Amber in a big way when Simon twisted Amber's words to make Montana think she had asked him if he'd 'rip her clothes off'. This, unsurprisingly, caused a huge rift between the girls, who ended up screaming at each other across the living room. Thankfully, the whole thing was cleared up quickly and thus the chain was broken.

OLIVIA - A LAW UNTO HERSELF

This girl could start a fight with a nun at church. Whether she was screaming at Chris for agreeing with her, yelling at Montana for asking her to calm down, having a go at Sam for sticking his fingers in pies or taking on Marcel for trying to help in an awkward situation, no one could escape Liv's fury. Our girl didn't need a chain, she was the whole blooming jewellery store.

FULL NAME:

Alex Beattie

NICKNAME:

Strong
But Silent

Alex

**Pre-Island
Occupation:**

Personal trainer

That explains the eight-pack he was flaunting around the villa!

celebrity lookalike:

A young
BRAD PITT

The floppy hair, the piercing eyes... Do they make men any more handsome than this?

Entered the villa

Day 26

fun fact

He loves eating 'sh*t food'. I guess that's fun to Alex.

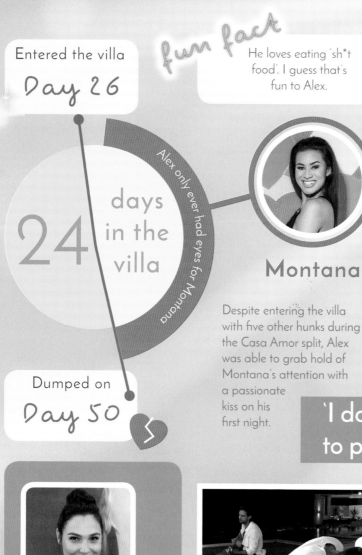

24 **days in the villa**

Alex only ever had eyes for Montana

Montana

Despite entering the villa with five other hunks during the Casa Amor split, Alex was able to grab hold of Montana's attention with a passionate kiss on his first night.

Dumped on

Day 50

KNOWN FOR:

BEING SILENT

He was the epitome of the strong, silent type – emphasis on silent. I suppose when you look like you've been sent from heaven, you don't really need the chat to back it up. And, as the last man standing from the Casa Amor split, Alex proved that looks really are more important than banter.

'I don't really know how to put it into words...'

MEMORABLE MOMENT:

Popping the Question

It might be memorable because he managed to string three sentences together, but we all let out a collective 'awww' when Alex popped the question. No, not that one – when he asked Montana to be his girlfriend. And looking at that beautiful face, of course she agreed.

celebrity crush: GAL GADOT

I mean, there's aiming high, then there's out of your league, and then there's trying to score with 'Wonder Woman' herself!

TYPE ON PAPER:

'Natural, clever and ambitious.' So, Montana.

Muggy Shots

Say what you like about them, but one thing our Islanders are definitely not is camera shy. But even when you're as fit as they are, it's still possible to be snapped from a bad angle. So, because it would be a shame to just delete them, and as a warning to us all of the dangers of being snapped unawares, here is a selection of the most jaw-dropping facial expressions of the series. From 'come to bed eyes' to 'I can't believe my eyes' eyes, here are the faces not to get caught with and the stories behind them.

CHLOE'S 'I LOVE TROUBLE' FACE!

Chloe may not have had the most malleable face in the villa, but she had no difficulty expressing her glee whenever there was trouble on the horizon. Specifically, the moment she twisted a casual comment from Mike into: 'Mike would drop Olivia in two minutes in the outside world.' Just look at her glee as the turd hits the turbine! We all love a bit of drama, especially when it involves someone else, but when millions of people are watching it's a good idea to try to control your delight – as hard as that may be.

OLIVIA'S 'OMG KEM HAS RE-COUPLED WITH CHYNA' FACE

The boys' mini-break to Casa Amor certainly stirred things up among our Islanders. Kem and Amber had been having a rocky patch, but it was the look of disgust on Liv's face as Kem walked back into the villa, arm in arm with Chyna, that became one of the mugshots of the series. If looks could kill, then Liv would be facing some serious jail time. In fact, she'd be a renowned repeat offender. So remember, when you do the dirty on your other half, you do it to their mates, too. Ain't that right, Liv?

JONNY'S 'WATCHING THEO STRUTTING HIS STUFF' FACE

The lesson here is 'don't wear your heart on your sleeve'. You would be forgiven for thinking that this was Jonny's 'I've just trodden in dog poo while wearing flip-flops' face, but in fact it is a face of pure green-eyed envy. Theo was showboating at the pool and Jonny was plotting to bring back the Nineties' term of abuse 'bellend' at the earliest available opportunity. It was a look that left us in no doubt about exactly what he was thinking. Unfortunately, those words are unprintable in a family-friendly book like this.

MONTANA'S 'ENJOYED AN INTIMATE MOMENT WITH ALEX' FACE

For this picture, it appears that keeping your partner happy in the sack requires a strategy of 'a little less conversation, a little more action'. Alex may not have been much of a talker, but from the look on Montana's face he was definitely a doer. It came as something of a surprise that slow burner Montana would go all the way with pretty boy Alex, but somehow he managed to turn up the heat, much to Montana's obvious delight. How did he do it? Probably by whispering sweet nothings in her ear – after all, he whispered everything else. Anyway, who cares as long as Montana is smiling?

AMBER'S 'TRYING TO CONVINCE HERSELF THAT CHRIS SAID SOMETHING HE DIDN'T BUT SHE THOUGHT HE DID' FACE

Similar in style to Chloe's mischievous misunderstanding (left), Amber took Chris's words and gave them a good old twist by claiming Chris had been cracking on to her. Chris was having none of it, but Amber had convinced herself she was right and was sticking to her story, no matter what. Is that the face of a woman who is making it all up? Actually, don't answer that... The moral of this story? Don't make stuff up about people – especially when everyone has the ability to rewind.

MARCEL'S 'I CAN'T BELIEVE I JUST KISSED SHANNEN' FACE

In reality, the person with the shocked expression on their face in this picture should be Shannen (remember her?). Poor girl. Who expects to be lip-locked from the blindside by a member of Blazin' Squad while playing an innocent game of Raunchy Races at Casa Amor? Aside from being one of the most unexpected and bizarre snogs of the series, it also caused some of the most trouble. The look on Marcel's face is a look that says, 'Oh dear, what have I just done? Gabby is going to kill me!' And she nearly did. So never forget, what goes on tour, doesn't always stay on tour!

The Ex-Files

Everyone had their favourite couples during the series, but what about the couples that you've forgotten even existed? In a villa where the action moves a mile a minute, the days turn to weeks, and last week might as well have been 2001! (Ahh, we'd all be wearing chokers and double denim... hold on!) It's hard to imagine that some of our favourite pairs had lives in the villa before they met each other, but let's go back a step and remind ourselves of the couples we've forgotten.

HARLEY & AMBER

While her future partner and fellow winner was cracking on with Chloe, these two got hot and heavy mere HOURS after coupling up. Amber was quick to leave Marcel in the dust as she stepped forward for hunky Harley on the first day. However, his lack of 'banter' spelled a swift end to their romance, followed by Harley's hasty departure from the Island. You may have been the first out, Harley, but along with Amber you also provided us with the first snog of the series.

OLIVIA & MARCEL

Cast your mind back to that first day in the villa, when none of our boys seemed to impress the incredibly picky blonde bombshell, Olivia. After initially sidelining our favourite former member of Blazin' Squad, Liv decided to forgo everyone else and couple up with a slightly brokenhearted Marcel. They may not have shared any romantic feelings, but they both made it all the way to the final.

KEM & CHLOE

Despite being mere metres away from the girl that he would eventually fall in love with, Kem's first coupling in the villa was with fellow Essex alumna, Chloe. Even though she had dated his mate in the outside world, Chloe was still happy to give Kem a go and vice versa. However, the pull of true love was too strong, and it was only a matter of days before Kem realized his dream girl was sleeping a few beds away.

DOM & TYLA

Yes, these two were once officially a couple! You may have missed it because they spent no real time together or had anything in common, but when Tyla first came into the villa she had Dom in her sights... Well, not really, but she was warned off Jonny and Chris by an angry female pack of Islanders. After a lukewarm date with absolutely no chemistry, the pair coupled up for all of four DAYS before they went their separate ways.

CAMILLA & SAM

Now this one seems made up, but we promise it was 100 per cent fact! Before Sam and Camilla did the rounds of the villa, they were initially promised to each other. Things started to turn sour when Camilla found out that Sam was 21, before revealing that she was... not 21. Sam swiftly turned his attentions to Liv (yeah, that happened, too!), before eventually being turfed out of the villa altogether. Temporarily anyway.

JONNY & DANIELLE

I know, we had forgotten about this one, too! During the sneaky 'twist or stick' re-coupling that followed Casa Amor-gate, Jonny decided to ditch Camilla and walk back into the villa with a beautiful blonde on his arm. He was quick to reassure a lonely Tyla that Danielle had just been his ticket back to the villa (charming), but in the official record books, these two were once an item.

MARCEL & MONTANA

Marcel's back with another girl-FRIEND! After failing to find anyone that they were romantically interested in, Montana and Marcel decided to save each other from being dumped by teaming up together. While we were secretly hoping that our one-time favourite boy and girl on the Island might go from friendzone to endzone, alas it was not meant to be. Luckily, Marcel would find his bae Gabby the following week, while Montana had to wait slightly longer for Alex.

LESSONS in love #7

Listen to your parents

They say that mother knows best - and, more often than not, it seems to be the truth. Parents seem to have a sixth sense about their children's partners, which often has no other explanation than their natural parental intuition. While Gabby tried to keep her cards close to her chest early on in the villa, it took her mum only two weeks to see that Marcel was 'the one' for her only daughter. It may have taken a little time and a few bumps in the road, but eventually Gabby was able to see what her mum had known all along and accept that Marcel was the only boy she needed in the villa. So, while you may need to teach your parents how to work their iPad or explain why they have a new speaking box called Alexa in their house, when it comes to matters of the heart, just do as they say.

FULL NAME:

Marcel
Somerville

NICKNAME:

Dr Marcel

Scan this QR code
on any smartphone
QR scanner app
to access exclusive
unseen footage of
Marcel

Marcel

Pre-Island Occupation:

He used to be in Blazin'
Squad but he doesn't like
to talk about it.

celebrity lookalike:

THAT BLOKE WHO USED TO BE IN BLAZIN' SQUAD...

What was his
name again?

Marcel claims to have slept with more than 300 women. Certainly a Fun Fact from his point of view! He was also in a celebrity couple with one of the girls from Vanilla Ninja (Google it, we had to).

KNOWN FOR:

BEING IN BLAZIN' SQUAD

Did we already mention he used to be in Blazin' Squad? Well, so did Marcel himself, over and over and over again. Despite claiming he wanted to keep it a secret, he accidentally told Jess, then Kem... and Sam... and anyone else with ears.

'Do you remember the Blazin' Squad?'

MEMORABLE MOMENT:

When No One Stepped Forward

That awkward moment which launched the series... He was the first man in *Love Island* history to fall at the first hurdle. Luckily, he managed to 'Flip Reverse' the situation and made it all the way to the final.

Gabby

Together for 45 days straight, Marcel and Gabby were the most stable couple in the villa

52 days in the villa

Montana

Olivia

Day 1
Entered the villa

Day 52
Fourth place

celebrity crush:

J LO

They're both musicians who were big in the Noughties so they're bound to have loads in common.

TYPE ON PAPER:

Before going into the villa Marcel said, 'I need to find someone who looks like an Instagram model.' Not asking for much, then. Still, I guess you came to the right place.

The movie business has the Oscars, the music industry has the Grammys and *Love Island* has these, the Muggys! The Muggys are the reward for seven weeks of pure - OK, not that pure - entertainment from the villa that makes the Playboy Mansion look like a nursing home for naïve nuns. All the Islanders were amazing during their time in the villa, but these awards are for outstanding achievements in their chosen fields, whether or not they knew it at the time.

So, without further ado, ladies and gentlemen, boys and girls, worldies and melts, may we present...

THE MUGGYS

Love Island

CATEGORY:

THE MELT AWARD
FOR ROMANCE

The first award is given for outstanding achievement in the art of romancing. This is the one that everyone wants to win, but with lines like, 'I'm not bovvered,' Chris didn't even make the shortlist.

THE NOMINEES ARE...

JAMIE FOR HIS BIRTHDAY BREAKFAST FOR CAMILLA

The way to a man's heart is through his stomach, and it turns out it works pretty well on women, too. As Jamie found out when he got up early on Camilla's birthday and lovingly carved out 'HAPPY BDAY CAM' in white, medium-sliced Hovis topped with some kind of homemade guacamole. It was a big risk – Camilla was as likely to correct his spelling and grammar as she was to appreciate the gesture. But it was pretty romantic. The only thing more romantic would have been for Jamie to have laid the food out on his own perfect torso for Camilla to feast on, like a gorgeous boy buffet!

KEM FOR HIS BRACELET PROPOSAL TO AMBER

The fact that Kem packed an infinity bracelet on the off chance of meeting someone in the villa that he wanted to spend infinity with does have more than a whiff of the pre-planned grand gesture about it. But that didn't stop it being one of the standout romantic moments of the series. Pass the tissues.

GABBY FOR HER DECLARATION OF LOVE TO MARCEL

Unwilling to show Marcel that she loved him through the traditional *Love Island* method of... you know... Gabby instead set about using her fellow Islanders to spell out the words 'I [heart] you' in size-zero model-sized letters on the lawn. However, did she really mean what she said using the contorted bodies of her friends? If the lie detector test is to be believed then the answer is no. Perhaps she just didn't have enough Islanders to spell out 'I quite like you'.

KEM FOR HIS PHONE TREASURE HUNT

Kem may have been the baby boy of the villa, but when it came to romance he was definitely the man of the house. Face it, he won the show and received a record two nominations in this category alone, proving his tactics are well worth noting. Take his 'find the phone' treasure hunt. Designed to win Amber's affections, it proved an absolute winner with the viewers, too. Not only did he get the girl, but he also bagged himself a few nights to remember. Go on, Kem!

AND THE WINNER IS...

KEM for his bracelet proposal

A hugely romantic moment, marred only slightly by Kem checking Amber understood what the word infinity meant before handing over the bracelet. Infinity, though! Even a wedding ring is only until 'death do us part', for crying out loud! Still, it proved a winning strategy and who'd have thought a pink shoelace could make a woman cry so much.

CATEGORY:

THE TOTES AWKS AWARD
FOR CRINGEY MOMENTS

There are always tricky moments in relationships. Those times when you just want the ground to swallow you whole. (And if the ground don't eat you, Montana will!) So, next up is the Totes Awks Award for all those cringeworthy occasions that made you want to hide away. Which is ironic, as some of these moments happened INSIDE the Hideaway.

THE NOMINEES ARE...

The Totes Awks Award

MARCEL FOR NO ONE STEPPING FORWARD FOR HIM

Despite being handsome, funny and big in the Noughties, Marcel was forced to suffer the indignity of being left hanging during the first ever coupling up. Still, with an enormous 300 notches on his bedpost there was probably nothing left of it, which means he could afford to wait. What a humiliation, though. If only the girls had known then that he used to be in Blazin' Squad!

SAM FOR STICKING IT ON MONTANA

Sometimes in dating it's possible to be too keen. A lesson Sam needs to learn if he's going to improve his technique with the ladies. It's no good being the charming, cheeky chappy if at the first chance of a snog you're all over the girl like a dog on heat. That's exactly what happened when Sam saw his chance with Montana and took it with both hands and a lot of tongue.

STORMZY FOR THAT TWEET

Not content with stirring up the music scene, grime legend Stormzy put the cat among the pigeons when he tweeted Chris some advice about Olivia: 'Chris you're too good for her (Olivia) mate.' Predictably, it went down like a cup of cold sick, but wasn't enough to split them up. Olivia got her own back on Stormzy with a sarcastic, 'Oh hey Babes', during the boys' rap masterclass. But it did serve as a reminder to Liv that it's possible to be 'Too Big For Your Boots' and sometimes it's good to 'Shut Up'.

GEORGIA FOR CHOOSING TO COUPLE UP WITH KEM

It takes a lot to make a bigger faux pas than appearing in public in tight white jeans, but Georgia managed it. If rocking up at a white party wearing a bright red dress wasn't bad enough, Georgia proceeded to fan the flames of the fire pit when she chose Kem in the re-coupling, stealing him from right under Amber's nose.

AND THE WINNER IS...

GEORGIA
for coupling up with Kem

Congratulations, Georgia, for playing a leading role in one of the most controversial re-couplings the show has ever seen. Not only that, but for making Amber see red and causing the first full-on face meltdown ever on national TV. And you thought wearing that frock was going to be the most daring move of the night. How wrong you were!

CATEGORY:

DRY YOUR EYES MATE
FOR BLUBBING

No awards ceremony is complete without a blubbing recipient, but this one is different because it's the bubbling that wins the gong. With so many tears being shed in the villa this year, this is one of **THE MOST** fiercely contested categories. There wasn't a dry eye in the house, well villa.

THE CRY BABIES, I mean nominees, **ARE...**

Dry Your
Eyes Mate

CAMILLA FOR CRYING OVER JONNY

Despite having dealt with warzones, when faced with losing Jonny to Tyla, the selfless, tough cookie Camilla reached breaking point, unleashing a tsunami of saline, the likes of which the villa has never seen. She even contemplated leaving, to allow the love between Tyla and Jonny to flourish. Little did she know that the producers had a bearded underwear model waiting in the wings to swoop in and sweep her off her feet. Although he'd need to be careful not to slip in the huge puddles of tears all over the floor.

TYLA FOR CRYING OVER JONNY

No doubt Tyla put Jonny's nose out of joint by cosying up to his arch nemesis, Theo, in front of his face, but she obviously still had feelings for the old grump. When Jonny was given the boot a few days later Tyla was left devastated. To make matters worse, Theo suggested that if she was that upset perhaps she should leave, too, leading to furious cries of 'kn**head' from Tyla.

DOM FOR CRYING OVER JESS

This was the unforgettable moment that Jess and Mike got dumped from the villa, tearing Jess away from her partner, Dom. Bamboozled by the news that his girlfriend of two weeks was heading back home, Dom broke down into a crumpled heap, moaning and wailing at the loss of his new love – although many fans took to social media to ask, if Dom really loved her that much then why didn't he leave, too? Hmmm.

CHRIS FOR CRYING OVER BABY CASH

Chris provided one of the cutest, funniest and most pathetic moments of the series when he lost it and started crying with love for his baby, Cash Hughes. As Chris showed, nothing is more powerful than the love for a child, even if that child is battery-powered and made of moulded plastic.

AND THE WINNER IS...

TYLA
for crying over Jonny

Congratulations, Tyla! You took it badly when Jonny fell on his sword to keep you in the game. We didn't know how you'd cope, but somehow you bounced back and found the strength to crack on with Muggy Mike within 48 hours of Jonny's departure. Well done, Tyla, you brave little soldier.

MUGGIEST
MOMENT
OF THE SERIES

Our final award was chosen **BY YOU**, the general public, via the *Love Island* app. It is, of course, the People's Choice award for the Muggiest Moment of the Series.

HERE ARE THOSE ALL-IMPORTANT NOMINEES...

Muggiest Moment

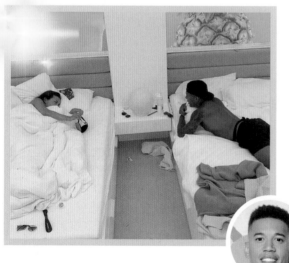

SIMON FOR TELLING AMBER HE WANTED TO RIP HER CLOTHES OFF

It's never the best idea to lie on the bed chatting with someone who isn't yours, saying you want to rip her clothes off. But that's what happened when Simon dropped the most unsubtle chat-up line on Amber in the history of *Love Island*. It caused a major drama between Montana and Amber. Luckily, they patched it up in the end, but Simon's saucy suggestion could have caused some serious damage.

THEO FOR TELLING TYLA SHE SHOULD LEAVE WITH JONNY

It was the moment when many began to think that maybe Jonny's comment about Theo being a massive bellend might actually hold some water. Tyla was devastated that her flame of two weeks, Jonny, had taken the decision to save her and sacrifice himself by leaving the villa, and so Theo sought to comfort her by suggesting that if she really had feelings for him then she'd leave as well. A flurry of tears, furious expletives and a stern word from Dr Marcel put Theo firmly in his place.

JESS FOR STEALING DOM OFF MONTANA

It was barely 24 hours that Jess had been in the villa when she started to shake things up. Given the power to couple up with any boy she wanted, Jess decided to steal Dom from Montana. Jess made out she felt bad about it but Montana was having none of it. The truth was that the two feuding beauties had a history, having dated the same guy on the outside. But it was Montana who had the last laugh when she bagged Alex, the prettiest boy in the villa.

MIKE FOR BEING MUGGY MIKE

It would be odd if the man nicknamed 'Muggy Mike' – a beacon of all it is to be... well, muggy – wasn't included in this category. He first earned the moniker when he coupled up with Olivia, much to Chris's annoyance, and the name stuck. Especially when he returned to the villa and set about trying to stitch up Olivia in revenge for mugging him off first time around. What a mug! Ridiculously fit, but a mug!

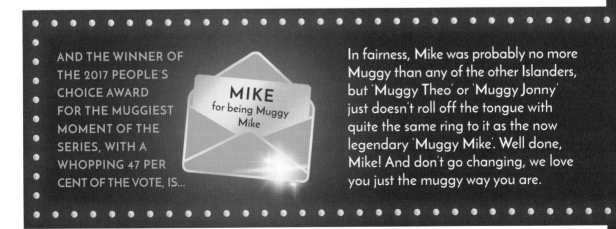

AND THE WINNER OF THE 2017 PEOPLE'S CHOICE AWARD FOR THE MUGGIEST MOMENT OF THE SERIES, WITH A WHOPPING 47 PER CENT OF THE VOTE, IS...

MIKE
for being Muggy Mike

In fairness, Mike was probably no more Muggy than any of the other Islanders, but 'Muggy Theo' or 'Muggy Jonny' just doesn't roll off the tongue with quite the same ring to it as the now legendary 'Muggy Mike'. Well done, Mike! And don't go changing, we love you just the muggy way you are.

FULL NAME:
Gabrielle Allen

NICKNAME:
Abs Fab

GABBY EXCLUSIVE!!!

Scan this QR code
on any smartphone
QR scanner app
to access exclusive
unseen footage of
Gabby

Gabby

Pre-Island Occupation:

Fitness instructor

She knows how
to get a man
motivated all right
- she had Marcel
running around
after her the
whole time.

celebrity lookalike:

SHARON FROM EASTENDERS

Maybe? OK, so
we struggled.

She once auditioned for a strip club but she didn't get through. Based on her moves in the villa, we would beg to differ!

KNOWN FOR:

NOT PUTTING OUT

Despite sleeping in the same bed as Marcel for more than a month, iron-will Gabs kept her clothes on and her legs firmly closed. Thankfully, Marcel was the patient type, and their old-fashioned romance took them all the way to the final.

There was no re-coupling for Gabby once she'd got her hands on Marcel

45 days in the villa

Marcel

All you need is one!

Day 7
Entered the villa

Day 52
Fourth place

'You could have slept with 1,000 people and still be s**t in bed!'

MEMORABLE MOMENT:

The Lie Detector

When the lie detector indicated that Gabby didn't love Marcel, wasn't looking forward to getting intimate with him and didn't believe he was the one, we were all baffled and bewildered. Luckily, the pair were able to put it behind them and move on stronger than before.

celebrity crush:
JUSTIN BIEBER

Just like Georgia, Gabs says that Biebs is the one she wants to call 'baby, baby, baby ooh'.

TYPE ON PAPER:

'Nice eyes, good jawline, strong head of hair, tall, defined body, strong legs, big hands, good dress sense, smart...' All right, love, it's a general type we were looking for not a bloody recipe!

Guide To

Relationships

#KeepItTogether

Guide to Relationships

Introduction

#KeepItTogether

Relationships are fluid. Or, to put it in a less new-age, hippy-dippy way, people change their minds all the time. How we feel in our relationships ebbs and flows, depending on all manner of factors – stresses at work, lack of sleep, finding naked pictures of your best friend on your partner's phone. That's the beauty of the *Love Island* villa. These real-world stresses and strains don't come into play, which means you get a purer, more concentrated version of what relationships are really like. There was a lot to learn from the way our winners, Kem and Amber, held it together through thick and thin. (He's thick, she's thin. Sorry, Kem!) The same can be said for Kem's bromance with Chris. You can say this for our winning man, the guy had all bases covered. Perhaps there's a lesson there for all of us?

Marcel, too, as well as being a loving (and patient) partner, still found time to divvy out hugs and advice to all who needed them. Something that we often forget about in relationships is that we all need our friends around us to help us become the couple we are or would like to be. For one thing, when you see the car crash that is your mate's love life up close, it can only serve to make you feel marginally better about your own disastrous relationship. Right, guys?

Be patient

As a curly-haired diva once sang, you can't hurry love! Just because you feel ready for the love of your life, it doesn't necessarily mean they are ready for you. Rather than rush into a relationship with Mr Right Now, chill out, pull up a seat and wait for Mr Right to come knocking. Just take a look at Montana. Sure, it may have been frustrating for her to keep kissing the frogs (very, very attractive frogs, mind you), but as soon as Prince Alex walked in she was ready to go. She only had to wait a month after her initial search, but we know that the real world moves a lot slower, so don't start panicking if you've been single for a year with no prospects on the horizon. As soon as the right one comes along you'll be off the market for good, so don't waste your 'you' time - enjoy being single while you still can.

KEMBER

The Winners' Story

He was the wild-haired barber from Romford and she was the drama queen from Wales, but after a roller-coaster 52 days of breakups, make-ups, showdowns and dramatic re-couplings, Kem and Amber emerged from the villa to a heroes' welcome as winners of *Love Island* 2017. Kem even announced to the world, 'I've met my future wife!' Let's hope so! A *Love Island* wedding? Now that would be a party to remember. There's no date yet, but Muggy Mike's already working on a strategy to stick it on a bridesmaid.

So what was their secret? How did these two Islanders manage to succeed where others failed? Well, it wasn't all plain sailing (despite Kem's sailor hat); our tempestuous pair split up on several occasions during the course of their summer of love. Nevertheless, the 'kemistry' between the lovebirds was undeniable way before they ever got it on. But before they could begin their romance proper, it was down to Kem to do what he does best. No, not a ladies' shampoo and set, but some serious grafting.

One major charm offensive later and Amber was well and truly under Kem's spell, dumping her original *Love Island* partner, Harley, and leaving the poor boy all revved up with nowhere to go but home.

Kem and Amber's relationship was always going to be a risky business. By his own admission, Kem had never had a proper girlfriend and Amber was nothing if not high maintenance. But, following their first kiss, it was clear they had potential, with Kem even admitting to Sam, 'I think I'm melting bad. Last night when I started kissing her I was getting goose bumps.'

Once the goose bumps had subsided, things cracked on apace, the grafting went up a gear and, just five days after deciding to couple up, the pair were making the traditional *Love Island* 'tent with one pole' in the communal bedroom. Actually, once they started their romping it was hard to stop them (TBH,

we didn't even try), and there was no confining them to the bedroom, either. On one occasion, after Kem confessed to 'getting a little bit excitable', the pair went in search of the perfect location for a bit of afternoon delight, checking out the dressing room, the balcony, the shower and the toilet before ending up 'doing the do' in Nathan's bed. Bad luck, Nathan! But at least somebody had sex there, eh?

As time passed by, the 'L word' began to loom and lust turned to love. Things were getting serious and this was cemented by one of the most romantic moments of the series, when Kem gave Amber his heart all tangled up in a cheap, pre-bought infinity bracelet, presumably from Romford market. No one could have ever imagined that a little bit of coloured string, purchased on the off chance before even entering the villa, could develop such symbolic significance. But despite what the sceptics said, 'that bracelet' secured Kem and Amber as a villa power couple and one of the main pairs to beat. Yes, it may be little more than a bit of old string, but when it comes to gifts it's the thought that counts*.

*Depending on who the recipient is, this isn't strictly true. Trust us.

Unluckily for them, the path to true love never did run smooth. And with this being *Love Island*, that particular path was more of a dirt track strewn with broken glass. This was the rough patch to end all rough patches. Kem decided he couldn't be himself around Amber, which drew her to the conclusion that she and Kem were totally wrong for each other. Mind you, she soon changed her tune when they split up and Kem started spending some serious time with new arrival, Tyla.

Amber might have been angry at Kem's ability to just move on, but her outbursts were nothing compared to the meltdown we were about to witness during the epic incident that historians are already referring to as 'The Chyna Crisis'.

It was all Casa Amor's fault! Everything would have been fine if it hadn't been for that pesky second villa. It was the ultimate honeytrap and the boys fell for it hook, line and sinker – especially Kem. It was supposed to be a civilized lads' day out. That was until Casa Amor was invaded by an army of superfit worldies with black belts in grafting.

Caught on the receiving end of such a sexy ambush, the boys didn't stand a chance and pretty soon Kem was being seduced by the exotic charms of Chyna. An incriminating postcard showing Kem and Chyna kissing ensured that wherever he'd slept at Casa Amor, back at the villa he was well and truly in the doghouse.

Things were so bad that both Kem and Amber chose to re-couple in the 'stick or twist' challenge. Kem re-coupled with Chyna, and Amber, in order to call Kem's bluff and save herself from being dumped, hooked up with Nathan, who she'd barely even spoken to. Seriously, there have been blind dates where the couples know more about each other than Nathan and Amber!

It seemed like love's young dream had got old and decrepit, but Amber was determined to fight for her man. After a romantic heart-to-heart when she shared exactly how she really felt, they decided to give it another go. Kember was back and, unlike most sequels, this second outing would prove to be even better than the first.

Things started going from strength to strength, and Kem proved himself to be quite the Casanova, organizing a smartphone treasure hunt around different spots in the villa that represented a milestone in their whirlwind love affair. And before you ask, no, Nathan's bed was not one of the spots.

With their relationship finally starting to get serious, it seemed like Kem and Amber were firmly on the road to victory. What could possible go wrong? Georgia, that's what. Trouble comes in many different shapes and sizes, and on this occasion it came dressed like a character from a Chris de Burgh song (ask your mum). 'Lady in Red' Georgia not only didn't get the memo about the dress code for the white party, she also failed to read the signals between our leading lady and her man, opting to bag Kem for herself in the most shocking re-coupling of the series – maybe ever.

In fairness to Georgia, she didn't really mean any harm and thought Amber would understand. Amber didn't, of course. Still, love conquers all and it wasn't very long before Georgia had ditched the bad red frock and found herself the eminently more available Sam, meaning that Kem and Amber were back on and back in the game!

The lie detector only served to confirm what we all already knew, that Cupid's arrows had made a direct hit and Kem and Amber were the real thing. They had become an unstoppable force, loved not just by each other, but also by the whole nation. As sure as eggs is eggs (even if they are all in the same basket), come the final Kember were crowned winners of *Love Island* 2017 and pocketed a cool £50,000 between them. And even when given the chance to steal the money all for himself, honourable Kem did the gentlemanly thing and opted to share it straight down the middle with his newfound 'bae'. Who knows what the future holds for our *Love Island* winners? A place in the country? Wedding bells, perhaps? Or maybe the pitter-patter of tiny feet? Whatever they do with all that money, I just hope Kem buys himself a new hat.

LESSONS in love #9 — Put all your eggs in one basket

We may have heard every single Islander giving us the opposite advice, but sometimes you need to lump all your eggs into one perfectly proportioned basket. Sure, that basket may be a little frayed around the edges, but that's what makes it the one for you. After cracking on with Gabby, Marcel never thought to spread out his eggs... Hmm, this metaphor might be losing momentum. Basically, Marcel decided to put all his charms and efforts into one beautiful blonde and it worked out an absolute treat. He didn't play the field, he didn't wait for someone 'better', he realized that Gabby was the best – and the rest is *Love Island* history!

Kem & Chris

The Ultimate Love Island Couple?

Over the course of the series there was one particular couple whose relationship seemed to stand the test of time. No, not Kem and Amber but Kem and Chris, or as we prefer to call them, Kis.

Love Island, as the name suggests, is supposed to be all about finding a love match, and there is one very important loophole - the bromance. Kem and Chris (we've given up on 'Kis' already) exploited that loophole to within an inch of its life.

Turns out, despite her concerns, Amber had nothing to worry about from the other girls in the villa; her major threat came in the form of everyone's favourite polar bear. From early on it became obvious that if Amber wanted Kem, she was going to have to share him with his BFF, Chris. People even started saying that it was those two who should be sharing the £50,000 prize money. But just how close did our brothers from another mother really get to each other?

PUBLIC DISPLAYS OF AFFECTION

Kem and Chris had no problem with the old PDAs; they loved each other and didn't care who knew. As well as finishing each other's sentences, Chris and Kem enjoyed sharing each other's beds, too. They loved nothing more than curling up in the sack for some pillow talk and a nice bit of spooning. But as we all know, it's only a matter of time before spooning leads to forking, or at the very least kissing.

It was so romantic! They were playing a game of beer pong in the garden, when one thing led to another and before anyone knew what was happening Kem and Chris were snogging in front of the whole villa, with tongues!

PRIVATE DISPLAYS OF AFFECTION

If snogging in the garden was a PDA too far, what the boys got up to in private was their own business. You see, Chris and Kem weren't just faking it for the cameras, their relationship was as close as any couple's in the villa. They literally had each other's backs when they started showering together and clearly enjoyed getting to know each other's bodies intimately. Who could forget Kem helping Chris measure his schlong or Chris speaking lovingly about Kem's 'little jelly baby'?

The pinnacle of their private relationship must have surely been when, in an act of bizarre male bonding, they shaved their initials into each other's pubes. But what is more shocking, how intimate the boys got or the fact that anybody in the villa still has pubes? Didn't they disappear in the Nineties?

A FAMILY AFFAIR

Not content with being Kem's BFF in the villa, Chris wanted to be part of his family on the outside, too. Kem had already asked Chris to be his best man, so when Kem's mum and brother popped around for a visit, Chris set about ingratiating himself with the family even further, inviting himself over for Sunday lunch without waiting to be asked. Fortunately, Kem's mum loved Chris almost as much as Kem did, saying, 'I think he's my third son now.'

A huge compliment indeed, but it did make things a little awkward with Kem's other, sorry, actual brother, Izzy, who admitted he found Chris a little intimidating. To be fair, who can blame him? With Chris in the picture, the position of Kem's best man at the wedding is now up for grabs. Poor guy. Still, think of the wedding pictures – Chris is ridiculously handsome.

WINGMEN

Having each other made going out and finding a partner easier for Chris and Kem. They shared information, dressed like twins and offered each other completely useless advice on pretty much everything.

They also looked out for each other, like the time Kem calmed Chris down when he started getting worried about Liv's flirting with Mike. Similarly, when Kem was feeling low during one of his brief breaks from Amber, Chris launched a mission to try and help his mate rediscover his mojo.

Their one-to-one chats provided some of the funniest moments of the series, and their carrot and hummus metaphor for cracking on means millions of people will never be able to fully enjoy crudités again. But perhaps the sweetest moment was when Kem nursed his poorly friend back to health, saying, 'I feel like someone has taken half out of me and I'm walking round with half a person.' You want to hope Amber and Chris aren't ever ill at the same time, Kem, or there'll be nothing left of you.

There hasn't been a *Love Island* wedding yet, but we can quite imagine these two happily married and settled down before any of our other lovebirds. It's only a matter of time before we hear the pitter-patter of tiny feet. Kem's probably.

Straight From the Heart

The Islanders' Vows!

Earlier in this book we mentioned all the bizarre ways our Islanders attempted to articulate their love for one another (see page 74) – Gabby's throwing shapes on the lawn, Marcel's lucky dip in a jam jar, Liv's infamous list – but this time it was serious. It was the *Love Island* vows, for crying out loud, a quasi-religious ceremony that, to *Love Island* uber-fans, is more important than any church union. These commitments had to hit the mark as millions had tuned in to hear them.

It's easy to get lost for words when trying to tell someone you love them, so why not take help and inspiration from these beautiful sentiments of our finalists.

The Girls' Vows

Gabby to Marcel

Marce... since the moment I met you, it's been an ever-growing connection I could never have contemplated I'd find.

Every time you catch me just looking at you and smiling, I'm counting my lucky stars that I met you. I'm blessed to have you in my life.

I'm honoured to be with someone who is respected and appreciated, and your love for your family and their love in return, it's so magical and rare.

We go from strength to strength daily, which gives so me much excitement and confidence in what the future holds.

It's been a long time coming, but right now I'm especially excited for you to 'Flip Reverse' it.

You're a dream come true and I love ya.

Some beautiful words there, but all most people at home were thinking was 'Get a room!'

Amber to Kem

Kem... when I walked into the villa I had no idea how much this experience was going to change my life. It is safe to say we've had one of THE most challenging journeys.

I wouldn't change any of those bad days we had because it made me realize I'd found something in someone that I didn't know was possible to find.

You have no idea how lucky I feel that you have made me your girlfriend, and I still think it's crazy that I've met someone who's literally the boy version of me.

I honestly love you with all my heart.

'Literally the boy version of me' – so basically, you're telling us your ideal man is you?

Olivia to Chris

Chris... the girl who walked into this villa seven weeks ago is a very different girl to the one who's walking out, and you are the reason for that.

You're cheeky, funny and the way you love me has brought out a softer side I haven't wanted to show in a very long time.

Your beautiful face matches an equally beautiful soul.

I always thought I knew what I wanted, but I never knew it would be a rapper boyfriend from Cheltenham and baby called Cash Hughes.

I know I could probably live without you, and probably live a lot longer for it, but after spending these last weeks with you, I know I never want to.

I honestly wouldn't change anything about you and I am totally in love with you.

Sweet and sarcastic at the same time. That's a first!

Camilla to Jamie

Jamie... at the time you arrived in the villa I thought my romantic journey on *Love Island* was over. I truly believe there is not a single other person who could have walked through the door to make me change my mind. I am humbled on a daily basis by your ability to bring out the best in others. And since you have been in the villa, I've been able to show sides of myself to you that I have kept hidden for a very long time.

My dad told me how happy it has made him to watch someone make me so happy. And that's really what it comes down to – I'm the happiest I have ever been because I'm lucky enough to meet a person who not only accepts me as I am, but has also helped me accept myself. And I couldn't adore you any more for that. Thank you – not only for completing my *Love Island* experience and making it the perfect journey, but for making me so excited for the future. There is no other person I would want to share it with than you.

A standing ovation from us. As Kem heckled, 'Stunning!'

The Boys' Vows

Marcel to Gabby

When I look back at our journey together, there are so many small moments that mean so much to me because without these smaller moments, this massive moment wouldn't be happening.

Whether it's our first kiss on the steps, or the bees interrupting us in the Hideaway, or your faith in my return from Casa Amor. At that point I knew I was falling for you.

Right now, I want you to close your eyes and try to think of all of our moments in here. Now snapshot each one of them in your head and put them together like a mosaic. And if you zoom out of that you should be able to see a bigger picture, which is me and you standing here after six weeks declaring our love for one another... and I love you.

Hang on... go back a bit. Shut our eyes and then zoom in, take a snapshot, make a mosaic... what? We're well confused.

Kem to Amber

So I walked in this villa, not a clue in the world,
That the girl of my dreams was actually a real girl.
I walked down them stairs and she had a guy
    by her side,
So as I walked past her I gave her a cheeky,
    'You all right?'

From the moment we started talking I got this
    amazing vibe,
She's so cute and funny and has got these
    ridiculous green eyes.
We would talk about our lives and the things we
    had been through,
It's mad to meet a girl who's so caring and true.

The relationship got rocky and we both
    started to fear,
The problem was we were scared to show we care.
The thought of being vulnerable was pushing each
    other apart,
When you find a girl that's special, you have to
    follow your heart.

Nice one, Kem. You pulled the heartstrings and managed to rhyme 'amazing vibe' with 'ridiculous green eyes'. Respect!

Jamie to Camilla

There are so many reasons writing something like this is so hard. Yet when you come to my mind, it's so easy to think of all the amazing ways in which to describe you. And this may seem like a contradiction, but the most endearing thing about you is you're exactly that, the amazing contradictions in your character that make you so special. You have the amazing ability to put others at ease in situations where you yourself admit feeling so uneasy. The amazing ability to see the beauty in everyone you meet, whilst ignoring the fact that you yourself are so beautiful.

The main reason this is difficult to write is fear. Just as you work so hard toward equality and justice in all parts of the world, I fear that no words that I could write could ever do justice to the unbelievable person you really are.

> Hang on, is he talking about Camilla or Nelson Mandela?

Chris to Olivia

Right... She turns heads, you can see that from tonight, and it's crazy how we fit and I can honestly say, hand on heart, I met the most amazing girl imaginable and the future excites me. I wrote a little poem called – 'Olivia'.

Our journey is ending, where another will begin,
And to me you're Snowy, if I was Tintin.

Your cuddles in the morning and your kisses at night,
But your freckles are one of my favourite sights.

So thank you for your love and allowing me to
    show mine,
I'm sorry for the arguments, I promise things
    will be fine.

And I love you.

> Nice one, Chris. It's amazing you made it to the end without Olivia taking the p*ss!

FULL NAME:

Olivia
Attwood

NICKNAME:

The F**kboy
Whisperer

Scan this QR code
on any smartphone
QR scanner app
to access exclusive
unseen footage of
Olivia

Olivia

Pre-Island Occupation:

Model

We never would
have guessed!

celebrity lookalike:

NICOLA MCLEAN

A model with a
vicious tongue...
I can't see the
similarities at
all, Liv.

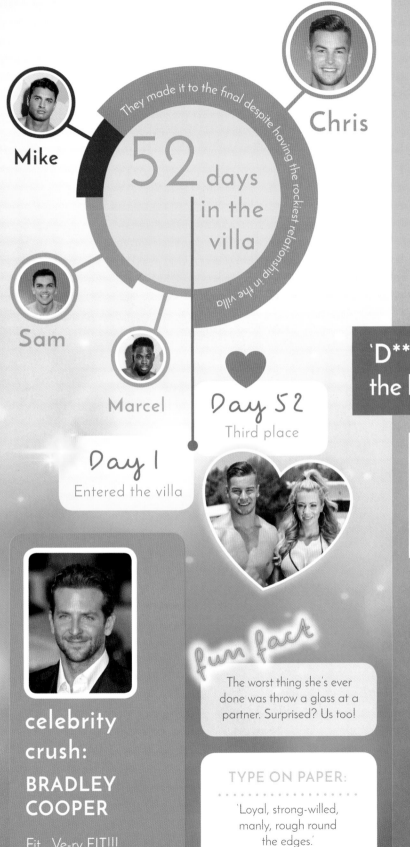

Mike

Chris

52 days
in the villa

They made it to the final despite having the rockiest relationship in the villa

Sam

Marcel

Day 52
Third place

Day 1
Entered the villa

**celebrity crush:
BRADLEY COOPER**

Fit... Ve-ry FIT!!!

fun fact

The worst thing she's ever done was throw a glass at a partner. Surprised? Us too!

TYPE ON PAPER:

'Loyal, strong-willed, manly, rough round the edges.'

YELLING... A LOT!

Whether it was aimed at Chris, or Montana, or Chris, or Sam, or Chris... Hurricane Liv was a force to be reckoned with. Take cover, she's about to blow... and not in the good way!

'D**ksand is back in the building!'

MEMORABLE MOMENT:

The D**ksand

First it was Sam, then it was Chris and finally Muggy Mike. The d**ksand took on many forms, but was always deadly to our Liv. Let's hope she stays safe out there.

ASK DR MARCEL!

Everyone in the villa has baggage. Just look at the size of those suitcases! But it's not that kind of baggage we're talking about, it's the emotional variety. The usual trials and tribulations we all struggle with in life, like unpaid bills, consumer issues or the love of your life sneaking off behind your back for a knee-trembler with a beautiful, yet predatory, horndog.

Luckily for the Islanders, there was good counsel on hand in the form of Blazin' Squad's wisest member, Dr Marcel, and now he's here to help you, too!

If he hasn't got an answer, he'll still give you a massive hug because that's just the kinda guy he is. It's time to – Ask Dr Marcel!

Dear Dr Marcel,

A mate's mum has been in touch to say my girlfriend has been spotted getting close to someone else. The paranoia is killing me. What should I do?

Yours,
Worried. Crosby,
Merseyside.

DR MARCEL SAYS...

We had a similar problem in the villa when Gabby's mum called to say that Mike was rumoured to be 'getting it on' with Jess. As I said to Dom, the choices are simple; sit it out and speak to her when you see her or move on and set about having some hot rebound action. I'd say the same to you; wait and worry or crack on with one of your flatmates.

Dear Dr Marcel,

Me and my girlfriend have been going steady for a while now and we're both really into each other. Yet try as I might I can't seem to convince her to 'seal the deal' in the sack. It's very frustrating and I'm more backed up than the M25 on a bank holiday Monday. Do you have any advice?

Yours,
Roger Stiff, Newport, S Wales.

DR MARCEL SAYS...

I feel your pain bruv, trust me, I've been there. I tried everything, but in the end you've just got to sit it out and if you think she's the one, it will be worth it in the end.

Dear Dr Marce,

I've recently split up with my boyfriend of five minutes using the classic 'It's not you, it's me' speech. All my friends think I've been a total bitch. What should I do?

Yours,
Ms F Boy-Whisperer,
Cockermouth, Cumbria.

DR MARCEL SAYS...

This is a problem I've seen before. Liv kicked Sam into touch totally out of the blue, telling him, 'You're irritating me but you're not doing anything wrong.' Poor Sam was humiliated and it caused some massive fights. My advice is if you want to split up with someone, don't confuse being honest with just being plain rude.

Dear Dr Marcel,

I am a huge fan of early Noughties British hip-hop and, try as I might, I have been unable to get my hands on an original copy of Blazin' Squad's 'Flip Reverse'. Can you help?

Yours
Mr S Tormzy, East London.

DR MARCEL SAYS...

No problem, mate. I've got a massive box of them under the bed at my mum's house. Pop round, you can have the lot for a fiver.

Dear Doctor Marcel,

I'm staying in a one-bedroomed luxury villa with 15 different people. I'm a bubbly blonde with a great personality but there's a problem. Every single boy in here likes girls with brunette hair and I haven't got brunette hair. I feel like asking for some hair dye. I'm actually not joking, by the way! Everyone literally fancies the brunette girls. Literally. I'm not being funny, they need to bring some boys in here who like blonde girls.

Yours,
Anonymous Blonde, Essex.

DR MARCEL SAYS...

Chloe, is that you? I know you were complaining about this last summer, but both Chris and I partnered up with blondes in the end, so maybe there was another reason you weren't successful in love? Just a suggestion...

If you'd like to ask Dr Marcel a question you can write to him at Love Island, The Villa, Mallorca, Spain. But no postcards! After the Casa Amor debacle Marcel has no time for postcards.

THE Love Island MORAL COMPASS

It was a jungle out there for our Islanders. Actually, it was more of a five-star apartment with an infinity pool – but morally, it was a jungle.

All series we saw our Islanders trying and failing to wrestle with personal ethical conundrums without any tools to navigate them through. Not any more. Now, neither you nor our Islanders will ever get emotionally lost again, thanks to this – the Love Island Moral Compass.

With your moral compass to hand, you will never make another muggy decision.

IF YOUR LIFE IS A MORAL MINEFIELD THAT EVEN CAMILLA COULDN'T DIFFUSE, THEN ORDER YOUR LOVE ISLAND MORAL COMPASS NOW!

ONLY £399.99

+ VAT + postage and packaging + 87% APR per annum.

Driven to crack on with the fittest person in sight, even though they have a partner? Sounds like a very Muggy Mike thing to do, but double check with your faithful compass – it just might be the right direction for you.

CHEAT

If, like Olivia, you're tempted to nip off and have sex in the Hideaway with Mike behind Chris's back, but aren't sure it's the right thing to do, simply refer to your moral compass to find out the morally correct course of action.

MUGGY

RE-COUPLE

SNAKEY

If, like Theo, you're drawn to the idea of winding people up and stealing their girlfriends (sound familiar, Jonny?), be sure to cast your eye over your pocket-sized ethical barometer before taking the leap.

PURE

If things are going west in your relationship and you can't work out whether to dump your partner for the new model you've just picked up at Casa Amor, don't follow your heart, consult your trusty instrument and follow the arrow.

Worried about your mum seeing you 'getting jiggly' on the telly, like Gabby? Simply check your moral coordinates on the compass and follow her virtuous lead.

The Do-It-Yourself
Lie Detector Test

The Islanders may have had a knack for bending the truth, but there was one thing they could never fool, the lie detector. Being strapped to a monitor and forced to answer intimate questions that revealed their deepest, darkest desires was always going to cause a bit of drama, but no one could hide from the truth. However, not everyone has access to Jeremy Kyle's props cupboard, so if you want to know if your partner is feeding you a batch of freshly baked lies, you'll have to be a little more sneaky about it. Here are some scientific-ish ways for you to work out if someone is guilty of telling porkies.

THEY COVER THEIR MOUTH

This is a physical sign that someone doesn't want to answer your questions - they are literally closing off communication. This was a textbook case, when Amber 'misunderstood' Chris's words and told Kem that he had been trying to crack on with her. As she was relaying the details to Kem, Amber instinctively covered her mouth, obviously realizing that her lies may be starting to catch up with her. Covering their mouth means someone isn't revealing everything, so it's definitely a sign to look out for. Unlike Kem, you won't have hundreds of hours of footage to trawl through to find the truth.

THEY STARE YOU DOWN

While it's common for someone who is lying to avoid your gaze, another thing to look out for is someone staring you down in an attempt to overcompensate. On his first night in the villa, Mike was confronted by Liv to explain why he had told Chloe that he would 'bin her off in two minutes', and his strategy was to lie his way out of it. He maintained eye contact with Liv in an attempt to control and manipulate the situation, obviously conscious that he was about to be rumbled. So, just because they are looking you dead in the eyes, it doesn't mean they're being truthful.

THEY REPEAT WORDS OR PHRASES

Chris's plan to convince everyone that he wasn't 'bovvered' about Muggy Mike's return to the villa was to repeat the phrase, 'I'm not bovvered,' to anyone who would listen. Suffice to say, he was bovvered, and him repeating himself was a sure sign to everyone that he was lying. Chris's repetition was an attempt to convince Liv, by convincing himself of his own lie. He was trying to validate the lie in his own mind and repeated the phrase so he could have time to gather his actual true thoughts. Sorry, Chris, you weren't fooling anyone!

THEY MOVE THEIR HEAD QUICKLY

It was a head-turn so quick she could have given herself whiplash. After returning to the villa, Sam directly asked Tyla if she and Jonny had ended things for good. She immediately changed her head position, which is an indication that someone is about to lie. Being forced to give a yes or no response to a simple question shocked Tyla, and her swift head movement before answering can be interpreted as her knowingly falsifying her answer. A liar will often jerk their head before they respond to a question, so look out for that dramatic head-turn, because we all know that in this case Tyla definitely wasn't telling the truth.

THEY CAN'T GET THEIR WORDS OUT

If you confront your partner about a situation and they start babbling like Boris Johnson at a press conference, the red flag is firmly waving. This happens because your mouth dries out during times of stress, making it harder for you to speak. Take a look at Simon. After being confronted about his flirtatious behaviour with Amber (saying he'd like to rip her clothes off), Montana forced him to explain himself. Instead of keeping calm, he panicked and within seconds he was struggling to put two words together, let alone sentences, and ended up completely fluffing his lines (or should that be lies?). So if they're struggling to get their words out, chances are they're struggling with the truth and there's a serious hole in their story.

FULL NAME:

Chris
Hughes

NICKNAME:

Polar Bear

Chris

Pre-Island Occupation:

Ambassador*/
farm boy

* for a golf
clothing company

celebrity lookalike:

PETER ANDRE MIXED WITH CRISTIANO RONALDO AND AN ICED GEM...

Is that a polar bear?

Chris doesn't feel like he's got the most out of a session unless he's snuck a finger up his partner's... um... 'hideaway'. So that's why Liv was always so angry!

Olivia

After winning Liv's heart, Chris stayed loyal until the end

48 days in the villa

Chloe

Day 4
Entered the villa

Day 52
Third place

celebrity crush:
EUGENIE BOUCHARD

The Canadian tennis player is tall, slim, blonde and, like Liv, will leave you needing new balls.

TYPE ON PAPER:

'Brunette, natural boobs and a good sense of humour.' Well, one out of three ain't bad. Having grown up on a farm, he's probably pleased to see Liv can handle a fair amount of sh*t.

KNOWN FOR:

HIS ONE-LINERS

From comparing himself to a 'fridged Easter egg' to trying to buy 'garlicio' from the local market, the random comments from everyone's favourite innocent country bumpkin made listening to Chris just as enjoyable as looking at him.

'Hashtag looks, hashtag game, hashtag personality, hashtag everything.'

MEMORABLE MOMENT:

The Monologue

Who could forget Chris's dilemma? After less than a week in the villa, he had to face the hard fact that everyone fancied him. Poor fella - beauty is such a burden.

Meet the Parents

It's a milestone in any relationship, the day you have to put on your best suit, remind yourself not to swear, and go and win over your partner's parents. Or, if you're one of our Islanders, you throw on a bikini and get ready to chat to a complete stranger who's seen you fornicate with their child on national TV. Here are a handful of ways our Islanders impressed their other half's parents on the first meeting - and if this lot can do it, anybody can!

GOING THE EXTRA MILE

While he was already in their good books, Kem showed Amber's parents that he was the kind of man who would go the extra mile for their daughter when he dazzled them with his Welsh phrases. Not only did he seem genuine, but he also came across as a complete sweetheart and won over the whole crowd. Showing someone's family that you value what is important to them is a definite way of making a good impression. You look like a hero, and they will be thanking their lucky stars their daughter found someone like you.

BE A MARCEL

Now this one might be a little harder to achieve, but modelling yourself on Marcel would be a great way to win over anyone's family. Gabby's mum had seen Marcel handle himself with dignity, be respectful of her daughter and be the man of the house - she never stood a chance of not loving him. Even after he had revealed that he had slept with 300 women and used to be a rapper, Gabby's mum saw nothing but a halo over Marcel's beautiful face. What a guy!

WIN OVER THE SIBLINGS

Getting someone's parents on side is one thing, but once you get the siblings on board you're on the home stretch. Becoming best friends with someone's brother means... OK, we're struggling here. We admit it, we just wanted an excuse to put in a picture of Gabby's sexy brother. Mmmmmm...

Alex may have been a man of very few words, but what he did say was pretty much perfect. When he met Montana's mum and aunty he was sure to mention how much he adored her and loved making her happy. The main thing that a mum wants to hear is that you are going to be good to her daughter, so with this statement Alex smashed it. He even had Mon's mum telling her that she needed to be nicer to Alex and not take advantage of him. In one meeting, Alex was able to not only win over his girlfriend's family, but also bring them over to his side. Very good work. We could all learn a thing or two from him... when he actually speaks, that is.

LAUGH IT OFF

Poor Liv had a hard graft in the show, not just with Chris, but with his parents as well. After publicly screaming and swearing at their son in front of the world, she was understandably nervous about the impression she had already made on Chris's folks. But, Liv being Liv, she chose to simply laugh at herself. During the meeting there were a few subtle jabs about their relationship, but Liv was able to take responsibility for herself and chose to joke about the situation, rather than take it personally. In the end, she had everyone cracking up and was able to start her journey over to their good graces. Sure, you may not have got off to the best start, but there are always ways to win someone over, and making them laugh is the first step.

TAKE AN INTEREST IN THEM

Our Camilla was always going to be a boss when it came down to meeting the parents, and she made sure that she followed the first rule of a parental meet-up – make it all about them. Camilla was quick to ask Jamie's mum what she had thought about the whole experience, making sure she knew that her feelings were important to Camilla. While his parents may want to know all about you, it's always best to make them the focal point of the day. That way, not only do you look as though you are genuinely interested in their family, but you also come across as a good listener and someone who doesn't need to be the centre of attention – all good traits for a potential daughter-in-law. Top work, Camilla.

The Cash Hughes
Guide to Good Parenting

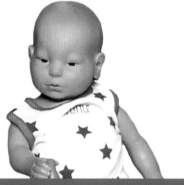

Hi, I'm Cash Hughes, son of Olivia and Chris. I may still only be a few months old, and don't seem to be growing at the same rate as other babies my age, but after spending some time in the villa under the watchful eyes of my loving mummy and daddy, I reckon I'm a pretty good judge when it comes to good parenting.

Now, I'm not saying that the other mums and dads weren't much good, but I did notice who took better care of me and my friends in the villa and whose efforts left a lot to the imagination. So I've taken it upon my good baby self to jot down a few ways they could improve when it comes to babysitting.

NAP WHEN YOU CAN

Us babies can be quite tiring sometimes, so you need to grab your shut-eye at every given opportunity. Harper's parents, Montana and Alex, took a very long nap in the middle of the day so that they wouldn't be too sleepy later on. Unfortunately, it sounded like Montana was having some nightmares as she kept moaning a lot, but when she finally got out of bed she seemed really happy. Even though Harper did cry a bit while they were asleep, they both returned to her looking very relaxed, if with slightly dishevelled hair. No idea why that was.

BE GENTLE WITH US

I like when my dad plays aeroplane with me, but when Uncle Kem does it with his baby I get a bit scared. He always holds his baby with one hand and it doesn't seem as though he is being very careful. If he fell down, the poor baby would get very hurt and I think Aunty Amber would be very cross. Uncle Kem is always fun to play with, but sometimes he needs to remember how small we are and be more gentle with us. I don't think it's just us, though, because Aunty Amber said sometimes he is rough with her, too – although she didn't seem to mind.

DON'T ARGUE IN FRONT OF YOUR BABY

Gabby and Marcel were usually really nice, but sometimes they would shout really loudly at each other, right in front of their baby. I even saw Gabby stick up one of her fingers at Marcel while she was holding her. I know my mum gets angry at Dad sometimes (OK, a lot), but they never yell at each other when I'm about, and if they did I would get very upset. Dad said it was just because Marcel was sensually frustrated – at least, I think that's what he said.

DON'T LEAVE US IN THE SUN

My daddy always made sure that I was wearing a hat and had factor 50 sunscreen on, but Star Sign's dad, Sam, wasn't very good at remembering that and always left her out in the sunshine. Even when people would remind him, he never listened and I was always worried that Star Sign would get sunburned. I am sure that he'll learn to do better, but Sam needs to start making sure that he doesn't leave Star Sign outside too long, especially when they're on holiday. Also, I didn't like it when they used to make me kiss Star Sign. I'm way too young to put all my eggs in one basket.

SPEND QUALITY TIME WITH US

It was really nice that Camilla and Jamie always liked to spend time together as a family. Even when Camilla had to go out for lunch with all the other mums, she was really sad to leave her baby, and Jamie made sure that she was never on her own. Part of being a strong family is spending quality time together, no matter what the activity. There is a line, though. My dad took me clubbing until 4am last night and I can still hear the bass ringing in my ears. Dad was super-tired by the end as he started slurring all his words and walking funny.

Island Guide

to Life

#LittleBitLeaveIt

Island Guide to Life

Introduction

#LittleBitLeaveIt

In many ways *Love Island* was more than just a television show. Indeed, it wouldn't be overstating it to say that it ushered in a new age of enlightenment. Well, we all certainly learned something. It's almost certain Chris had never seen an avocado until Jamie used one to make Camilla's birthday breakfast. We also learned that Mike's beauty easily matches that of Michelangelo's *David* and, rumour has it, he would need a much bigger fig leaf.

There has also been a renaissance of culture, thanks to our Islanders – art, in the form of their very own holiday selfies, and rap music, in particular. There was nothing Biggie about the Smalls worn by the girls in the villa, but the boys' rap classic 'Little Bit Leave It' has already earned a place in hip-hop legend.

All of the above will be addressed in this our final chapter. And, sticking with the scholarly theme, we've also included The Ultimate Love Island Quiz (see page 202) so you and your mates can test your knowledge and see how well you know the show. Maybe you could even use it as an icebreaker with that person you really fancy who you know also loves *Love Island*. Why not ask them over to play the quiz? What are you waiting for? Get grafting and start loving like a true Islander!

LESSONS in love #10 Absence makes the heart grow fonder

Not the most imaginative lesson we've got, but it proved true for our original *Love Island* lovebirds, Jess and Dom. Despite a magical 17 whole days together, the star-crossed lovers found themselves ripped apart when Jess got the boot and forced to live without each other for another nine days until Dom could join her. It's just like *Casablanca*. The homecoming was a rocky affair, due to Jess's did they/didn't they tryst with a certain Greek sex god, but they eventually found out that their love was stronger than ever. They even did a spread together for *OK!* magazine, which is a sure sign of deep devotion. Just because your individual paths may have forced you apart, it doesn't mean the journey is over. It may even take you to some fascinating and exotic places... like Devon (where Jess lives).

Educating Mallorca
Love Island Lesson Time

They say travel broadens the mind, but a short flight to Spain, only to be locked in a love shack for seven weeks, is hardly a gap year. As idyllic as the villa is, no one would argue it's the best vantage point from which to purvey life's rich panorama. That said, our Islanders didn't shy away from the occasional highbrow discussion and were constantly trying to better themselves. At times the villa felt more like Oxford, the city of 'dreaming spires' and ivory towers, than a state-of-the-art passion palace. Here are a few of the more impressive moments from the academic year.

SUBJECT: WELSH

When Kem chose to learn some Welsh to impress Amber's dad, he decided against the Chris strategy (see opposite) of just hollering a load of nonsense in Old Pa Davies's face and instead did his homework, learning a few basic Welsh phrases. It paid off. Sure, he had to read the sentences directly from his phone but the sentiment was there, meaning Kem was in the good books. Tidy, as they say in Wales, and proof of how useful a good education can be.

SUBJECT: HISTORY

On the night of the glitter party, while most of the girls were busy slut dropping like it was going out of fashion (was it ever in?), Olivia and the boys settled down for a seminar about evolution. There's no point trying to explain it. Here's an extract:

(Warning: If you are an evolutionary biologist of a delicate disposition, look away now.)

SAM: Is he [Jesus] related to God?
CHRIS: He's God's brother.
KEM: Before anything happened, the world was just a piece of land, yeah? And then fish came out the water with legs, dropped a sperm; somehow that sperm's gone into a person...
OLIVIA: When you get out of here, you need to go to the Natural History Museum.

Sage advice, Olivia, but you don't want to go during the summer holidays, the queues are horrendous. Fortunately, Jamie arrived a few weeks later and, with his beard giving him a passing resemblance to Charles Darwin, had his own stab at explaining evolution. He needn't have bothered. Sam and Chris refused point-blank to accept that a dolphin is a mammal, not a big fish, and poured scorn on Jamie for even suggesting it. So much for survival of the fittest. They might be fit, but they wouldn't survive five minutes in a biology class.

SUBJECT: ENGLISH LANGUAGE

Sam may have laughed in the face of scientific fact, but in fairness to him, how would he know? The only thing he's read are his tattoos and that was in a mirror, which, admittedly, is not easy. But the biggest lesson Sam should learn from his time in the villa is that he is not as clever as he thinks. He failed to spot the signs that Montana wasn't feeling it, saying, 'Let's see how much our love escalates.' He then went on to question the existence of the word 'escalates', despite having used it two seconds earlier. Do you want to tell him or should we?

SUBJECT: SOCIOLOGY

Love Island is all about men and women getting along, yet a battle of the sexes erupted during an excruciating conversation between Jonny and Camilla. As is the way in the villa, conversation had inevitably turned to politics and it wasn't long before a row kicked off when Jonny suggested that, basically, feminists need to get off their high horse (presumably with the aid of a chivalrous gentleman). Short of asking her to iron his shirt, Jonny couldn't have dropped a bigger clanger. Clearly taken aback, Camilla set about schooling the sexist pig good and proper, saying, 'I think it's difficult for men to see that there's been several generations which have been preferential towards men, and therefore to redress the balance, there has to be in some way an active movement towards equality.'

After she'd torn Jonny a new one, Camilla ran off and cried her eyes out to the girls. Crying over boys aside, Camilla's feminist stance served to cement her reputation as *Love Island*'s top boffin. Oh, and she knows how to diffuse bombs, too! Come on!

SUBJECT: SPANISH

If anything screams 'intelligent, serious, relationship' more than sleeping with each other on national TV, it's hosting a dinner party. It's what clever people do! Chris and Olivia were set the challenge of cooking a civilized dinner for their fellow Islanders. They chose a very exotic dish called Spag Bol, then headed to the local village to buy their ingredients. But first they had to brush up on their Spanish. Chris, having forgotten most of what he'd learned at school, thought on his feet and fell into the classic British trap of shouting what he wanted in English using a bad Spanish accent and adding the letter 'o' onto the end – 'garlicio', anyone?

Hey, Good Lookin', What You Got Cookin'?

Food and love have always had a close connection and our Islanders had a huge appetite for both. As the saying goes, 'A villa that eats together, sleeps together.' So if you're hungry for love, or just plain hungry, then here are a few *Love Island*-inspired recipes to impress your partner.

Chris and Liv's Spag Bol

Who can forget the night Chris and Olivia cooked up a lovely meal of Spag Bol for their fellow Islanders. It wasn't easy, as Chris's language skills made buying the ingredients harder than the actual cooking. Remember this hysterical exchange?

OLIVIA: What's a tomato in Spanish?
CHRIS: *Tomato... e*
OLIVIA: We need garlic?
CHRIS: *Garlicio, garlicio?*

Garlicio caused a storm on Twitter and confusion from the poor grocer, who wondered why a man with an iced gem on his head was shouting gibberish in his shop. Chris's terrible Spanish aside, the bigger worry is that neither of them knew the English for 'aubergine' and thought they were known as 'd**k emojis'. A moussaka will never taste the same again.

But never mind that, here's everything you'll need to make the perfect Spag Bol, Chris and Liv style.

INGREDIENTS:
1 medium *onionio*
2 cloves *garlicio*
500g *mincedio beefio*
1 tin chopped *tomatoes*
1 packet spag
Parmesanio cheeseio

METHOD:
Starting with the *onionio* and *garlicio*, fry the ingredients in a pan. Stir in the *tomatoe* and simmer for 40 minutes, trying not to have a row with your fellow cook.

Boil the spag in hot, salty water – maybe Camilla's tears? Then drain.

Add the *cheeseio* and serve with love, allowing 12 hours for the food poisoning to kick in.

Jamie's Smashed Avo on Toast

This now legendary breakfast spelling out 'Happy Bday Cam' in avocado on toast secured Jamie's place in Camilla's heart. Here's how to make the perfect superfood birthday brekkie.

INGREDIENTS:
1 loaf alphabet-shaped sliced white bread
1 avocado
1 dictionary (for spelling)
Butter

METHOD:
Take the bread, remove the letters required from the loaf, and toast. Mash the avocado and spread on the toast, ensuring you don't accidentally spell out a swear word or the wrong person's name. Serve wearing just your underpants (optional).

Melts

After Theo described Jonny as 'a tuna melt' and Kem called Theo a 'ham and cheese melt', melt became the go-to diss of the series, and now you can join in on the action, too.

INGREDIENTS:
Butter
1 loaf bread
1 pack ham or 1 tin tuna
Sliced cheese

METHOD:
Butter one slice of bread and place it buttered side down on a hot sandwich maker. Add the ham or tuna and top with sliced cheese. Butter a second slice of bread and place the unbuttered side on top of the sandwich. Close the sandwich maker and cook until the bread is toasted and the cheese has, well, melted.

Montana's Biscuit Surprise

The surprise in Montana's Biscuit Surprise is it's just a biscuit. Montana might have chosen a carrot to graze on while gazing at sexy new arrival, Mike, but she chose a biscuit to nibble on when Dom and Chris asked her whether they were better looking than him. With a mouth full of Hobnob, our girl Montana told them straight. This recipe is made for all you novice chefs out there, so be brave and give it a go.

INGREDIENTS:
1 packet Hobnobs/any other biscuit

METHOD:
Remove biscuit from pack and eat while gossiping about Island life. Repeat until stuffed or no one will listen to you any more.

Kem and Chris's Cruise Crudités

Chris and Kem's chat comparing girls to hummus has gone down in *Love Island* history. Amber was the 'hummus with the olive in it' and Kem wanted to try the other hummus (sans olive, aka Chyna). Chris was right behind him, telling him to get stuck in. Chris's advice turned out to be complete nonsense on every level but cemented the boys' bromance. So in case Chris and Kem's metaphor hasn't put you off hummus for life, here's how put together some crudités the Chris and Kem way.

INGREDIENTS:
Carrots (raw),
Hummus (without the olive in it)

METHOD:
Dip the carrot into the hummus.

FULL NAME:

Jamie Jewitt

NICKNAME:

Mr Perfect

Scan this QR code on any smartphone QR scanner app to access exclusive unseen footage of Jamie

Jamie

Pre-Island Occupation:

Model

And being a general model man!

celebrity lookalike:

DAVID GANDY

Just imagine being the filling between that beefy sandwich!

fun fact

Jamie is a massive science nerd. Yes, that kind of hunky nerd from an action film who ends up saving the world from an apocalypse with barely a strand of hair out of place.

Day 32
Entered the villa

20 days in the villa

Camilla

Day 52
Second place

KNOWN FOR:

BEING PERFECT

Whether you were gazing at his gorgeous face, watching him knock up a gourmet meal, witnessing him break up a row or checking out his perfect pecs, Jamie appeared flawless. He also loved reading and could talk geoglobal politics all day. Is there anything the man couldn't do?

'I was just working for Calvin Klein.'

MEMORABLE MOMENT:

Jamie and the Guitar

Just when we thought he had reached the peak of his perfection, Jamie pulled out his acoustic guitar and a matching set of soulful vocal chords. Seeing him in a crisp, white shirt, holding a guitar and singing a love song... well, if Carlsberg made boyfriends...

celebrity crush: CAMILLA THURLOW

Being too much of a gentleman to answer such a question before he entered the villa, we can only presume it was because he already only had eyes for his beloved Camilla.

TYPE ON PAPER:

Jamie doesn't have a type, he prefers personality. Of course he does, because he's perfect.

Island Politics

With a reality star already in the White House, there is every chance we may have a future Prime Minister in the villa. But of all the possible candidates, who would make the best politician?

Marcel

POLITICAL PARTY:
The Blazin' Squad

MAIN POLICY:
To 'Flip Reverse' it (whatever that means)

CABINET POSITION:
Health Secretary
(as a Doctor - what else?)

A pragmatic operator with the looks and charisma to go all the way to Number 10. He's already been to Number 1 in the charts and sold out Wembley Arena, which means he's starting off with a large base of core supporters. He's also recently come to the attention of Labour leader and *Love Island* fan, Jeremy Corbyn. If Marcel can think of a rap to go with the famous 'Ooh, Jeremy Corbyn!' chant, it could be his ticket to power. Maybe.

Camilla

POLITICAL PARTY:
The S.F.P (Scottish Feminist Party)

MAIN POLICY:
Trying not to cry

CABINET POSITION:
Secretary of State for Defence
(although, as a feminist, Camilla won't like being anyone's secretary)

A bomb-disposal veteran who has seen active service will go down well with voters in Middle England. However, Camilla's strong feminist principles could make her popular with the youth vote (and women, obvs). She's not afraid to show emotion but has an iron will. She also has the ideal First Man, Jamie, at her side. While Camilla makes boring speeches, we can bathe in Jamie's furry-faced beauty. If she makes it, Camilla would be the third female Prime Minister and the first to truly know how to rock a bikini. Camilla is a rare breed, a strong feminist who could both win with a landslide at the ballot box and make the earth move in the bedroom. Now there's a thought.

Theo

POLITICAL PARTY:
The S.N.P (Snakey No-gooders Party)

MAIN POLICY:
Winding everyone up

CABINET POSITION:
Secretary of State for Sport

Chloe

POLITICAL PARTY:
The E.I.P (Essex Independence Party)

MAIN POLICY:
To make Brentwood the nation's capital

CABINET POSITION:
Secretary of State for Gossip

If recent politics have taught us anything it's that voters appreciate a candidate who says it like it is. Step forward, resident villa loudmouth, Chloe. If there was one thing this girl loved, it was wagging her tongue around and spreading lies and false accusations like they were going out of fashion. Remember how she got the whole villa hating on Mike with her claims that he called Olivia a bitch when he clearly didn't? Hang on a minute – lies, false accusations, always squirming out of difficult situations when under heavy-fire questioning... Chloe sounds like the perfect politician.

Marino (who?)

POLITICAL PARTY:
The Who Hell He? Party

MAIN POLICY:
To be recognized

CABINET POSITION: Brexit Secretary
(Marino's exit had no noticeable effect on the villa or its inhabitants. What better man to put in charge of Brexit negotiations?)

A rank outsider! Marino was only in the villa for five minutes but he will have gleaned valuable experience. Like that French dude, Emmanuel Macron – he came from nowhere and now he's running the show. The worry is, with a name like Marino how's he ever going to win over the hardcore Brexiteers?

Mike

POLITICAL PARTY:
Nonstop 24 Hours Party

MAIN POLICY:
Sex free at the point of delivery

CABINET POSITION:
Chief Whip

A sneaky, duplicitous, sexy maniac? Mike is a born politician and WILL one day be Prime Minister. It's a surefire thing. Once they've looked into those eyes, people fall under his spell and would vote for absolutely anything he said. Being a perma-tanned sex ninja who sleeps with 90 per cent of the women he meets would have been political suicide 20 years ago. Not any more! These days it's an asset and a PR triumph. Who wants to read the headline, 'Prime Minister Found In Bed With Own Wife'?

A true Machiavellian political operator, Theo knows how to push people's buttons (thank God it's not nuclear ones). His constant needling of Jonny caused him to lose it and to leave the villa, to 'spend more time with [his] family'. If he put his mind to it, Theo could easily be Master of the Known Universe, but his acid tongue could get him into trouble. Also, his background as an athlete would be invaluable when running from disgruntled protesters.

LOVE ISLAND BANGERS

—

THE ULTIMATE PLAYLIST

If music be the food of love, then whack it on and crank up the volume! Whether they were getting over an argument or getting under another Islander, nothing set the tone quite like a perfectly placed tune. When it came to Island life, music brought the whole place together – mostly because it was much harder to argue when the stereo was booming out with Bieber on repeat. So if YOU want to party like an Islander in the comfort of your own villa (living room), then here are a few of the tracks the Islanders actually chose THEMSELVES as their must-have tunes for a banging night...

VILLA TUNES

FLIP REVERSE - Blazin' Squad
Added by Marcel
Did you know he used to be in the Blazin' Squad? He really should make more people aware.

DESPACITO (REMIX AUDIO) - Luis Fonsi, Daddy Yankee ft. Justin Bieber
Added by Kem and Amber
Let's hope Kem's Spanish is better than his Welsh.

FOREVER - Drake ft. Kanye West, Lil Wayne and Eminem
Added by Chris
Is this track an omen for Chris and Olivia's relationship?

LAPDANCE - N.E.R.D
Added by Gabby
About as far as Gabby went in the villa, much to Marcel's frustration!

INTO YOU - Ariana Grande
Added by Montana
And by that look on her face (see page 123) Alex certainly was.

ALL RISE - Blue
Added by Craig
It didn't matter how much Craig sung it, it just wasn't going to happen for him.

AFRICA - Toto
Added by Camilla
As if Mallorca wasn't hot enough!

MAKE YOU FEEL MY LOVE - Adele
Added by Tyne-Lexy
Sadly none of the Islanders did feel it and our TLC was quick to get DFV (dumped from villa).

NEEDED ME - Rihanna
Added by Dom
I hear that track was on a loop after Jess left the villa.

WILD THOUGHTS - DJ Khaled ft. Rihanna and Bryson Tiller
Added by Amelia
I bet those thoughts didn't include being dumped from Casa Amor
before even setting foot in the villa...

FULL NAME:

Camilla
Thurlow

NICKNAME:

Freak in
the Sheets

Camilla

Pre-Island Occupation:

Explosive ordnance
disposal

She managed to
dispose of a few of
our bombshells pretty
quickly... Sorry Craig!

celebrity lookalike:

Fellow princess
**PIPPA
MIDDLETON**

Now that's what
you call a right
royal lookalike.

Craig

Jonny

52 days in the villa

Jamie

Talk about saving the best till last!

Day 1

Entered the villa

Day 52

Second place

Sam

celebrity crush:
SONNY BILL WILLIAMS

He's an All Blacks rugby player and heavyweight boxer, so who are we to argue?

TYPE ON PAPER:

Camilla was so regal that we should really be talking about her 'type on parchment'. She enjoyed a bit of rough with Craig and got gruff with Jonny before opting for the smooth operator Jamie.

KNOWN FOR:
CRYING... A LOT!

Whether she was dating Jonny, getting over Jonny or having a feminist debate with Jonny, our Camilla knew how to turn on the waterworks. The cost of the water damage to the villa from her incessant blubbing is still being assessed.

'Lady on the streets, Freak in the sheets!'

MEMORABLE MOMENT:

The Liberation of Camilla

It may have taken Jonny four weeks for a boob grab, but Jamie didn't waste any time getting to work on Lady Camilla.

Villa Ice
How to Rap Like an Islander

While our Islanders may have been superstar DJs with their own party playlist (see page 183), a few also had their own talent for making music. It all started with a producer, Marcel, aka Rocky B, then came the 'talent', Kem, aka Lil'Kem, and finally the hype man, Chris, um...Vanilla Ice Gem? When these boys weren't in the studio (living room) with Stormzy, they were honing their craft by the fire pit or performing live to tens of people on the villa stage.

Oddly, the boys' original numbers didn't crack Spotify or the iTunes Top 10 list, but we couldn't let these musical masterpieces go to waste, so we got our hands on the boys' original lyric sheets. Now you, too, can sing along to the song of the summer. No, not 'Despacito' - 'Little Bit Leave It', of course. Scan the below code to spit some bars with the lads - we guarantee you'll have a right good grime!

Scan this exclusive QR code on any smartphone QR scanner app to re-watch the boys rap and sing along.

Little Bit Leave It

Music and Lyrics by
Marcel, Kem and Chris

CHRIS: Listen, listen
Little bit leave it
Kem, Chris and Marce
Big up Marce on production
Big up Kem on the feature
If you don't know, get to know, dun'kno
Us boys are gonna teach it
Marce, what you saying is a little bit leave it?

MARCEL: First day on the Island, ain't what I needed
No one stepped forward
That's a little bit leave it

KEM: Chloe said she liked me but did she really mean it
Fall back babe
You're a little bit leave it

MARCEL: Marce, I'm the gent in the villa
Gabs walked in and I'm onto a winner
Gab's wified, dropped in like a bombshell
Made a little one, two, steak for the dinner

First five weeks had too much fun
Energy between us second to none
In the final don't care where I come
Cause with this girl I've already won

First day on the Island, ain't what I needed
No one stepped forward
That's a little bit leave it

KEM: Chloe said she liked me but did she really mean it

Kem, I swear I'm five foot ten
I was on a hype when I first walked in
Then, I met this ten out of ten
Had a league one chick but my tings Prem'

21 years and I never had a chick
Then I met this girl, things just clicked
Thought we were done but rewrote the script
Now I've fallen in love, life's just lit

MARCEL: First day on the Island ain't what I needed

CHRIS: Cause Casa Amor was...

EVERYONE: A little bit leave it

Party Like an Islander

In many ways, the whole 52-day experience was one big party for our Islanders. We'd all love to have been there, but most of us can't just take all that time off, strip to our swimwear and spend seven weeks living it up in paradise. But we do have the weekends. So, with that in mind, here are some practical ways to host the ultimate *Love Island* party in your very own living room.

CHRIS'S PARTY PIECE

Everyone has a party piece. It's a crucial part of being the life and soul of the party. It can be anything – some people sing, some people can do impressions and Chris can fill a pint glass with his flaccid penis. Move over Noël Coward.

We got our *Love Island* willy experts on the case and they've reported back that a pint glass is 15cm deep. You can do the rest of the maths yourself. It also lays truth to the fact that polar bears are thought to have the biggest willies of the bear world. If there is any justice, this game will be in the next Olympics.

WHAT YOU WILL NEED: 1 pint glass (not the one you are drinking out of)*.
1 very large...

NUMBER OF PLAYERS: As many men stupid enough to give it a go as possible.

THE RULES: Take the pint/shot glass and... you get the idea.

*If none of the men in your group 'hit the mark' (bottom of the glass), then a shot glass will work just as well.

THE KISSING CHALLENGE

If you're hosting a *Love Island* bash then you'll want to make sure that any games you play are good fun and put romance firmly on the agenda. The Kissing Challenge is ideal for this one. It won't be weird at all. Camilla really enjoyed playing and described it as, 'Lots of fun. It was like some strange version of Countdown.' I'm not sure Rachel Riley would agree but it might make a great Christmas special.

WHAT YOU WILL NEED: Blindfolds and lip balm.

NUMBER OF PLAYERS: As many as you've got. Boys, girls, all welcome in this one. Although we wouldn't recommend playing it at a family party.

THE RULES: The boys stand in a line blindfolded and the girls make their way down the line snogging each boy and marking their kissing technique out of ten. The winner is the boy with the most points at the end.

WARNING: Beware of cold sores and rogue tongues.

SAUSAGE FEST

A *Love Island* classic, Sausage Fest will go down in history as the funniest and most inventive way to crowbar cheap innuendo into a TV show ever attempted. #NiceBangers. What's not to like? We got some very saucy telly and a brand new game to play with friends at the next BBQ.

WHAT YOU WILL NEED: Sausages. Lots of sausages. The Islanders made their own, but our advice is head to the nearest supermarket and fill your trolley with as many bangers as you can get your hands on.

NUMBER OF PLAYERS: Couples aged 18 to 80 (if they still have a bikini). The game is played by unlimited couples made up of one boy and one girl.

THE RULES: Like Chris, the rules are simple. The boys have 90 seconds to attach as many sausages to their partner's body as possible.

After you've tried it, you'll be hooked. Unless you're like Camilla, who, after playing for the first time, said, 'I've had enough sausage to last a lifetime.' (Jamie had something to say about that.) Play once and we're sure you'll agree with us – it's a great game and perfect for breaking the ice at any social occasion.

POLE DANCING

This game caused ructions in the villa, but seeing your mates in hotpants writhing against a broom handle for points makes it worth risking a massive row for.

WHAT YOU WILL NEED: 1 broom.

NUMBER OF PLAYERS: As many people willing to risk lifelong back problems to win a pointless prize as you can get.

THE RULES: Players must pole dance while answering questions*. Ideally these will be as personal and awkward as possible for the player to answer, like the one that floored Gabby: 'What percentage of the public think Marcel shouldn't have snogged twice during his time at Casa Amor?' Remember, playing this game is like playing with fire, but do give it a go if you've had enough to drink.

WARNING: Do not take part if you have back problems or dirty secrets.

*No reason for the pole dancing, really, but this is *Love Island* so OK.

FULL NAME:

Kem Cetinay

NICKNAME:

Lil' Kem

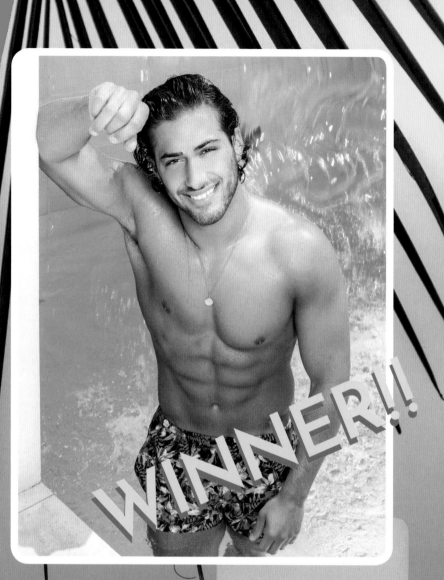

WINNER!!

Kem

Pre-Island Occupation:

Hairdresser and full-time mummy's boy

celebrity lookalike:

THE LOVE CHILD OF STACEY SOLOMAN AND JAMES 'ARG' ARGENT

Who's a lucky boy then?

SPITTING BARS

Kem may have made a living by using his hands but it was his mouth that had the nation captivated. His hits, like 'Little Bit Leave It' (see page 187), had the whole villa reaching for their earplugs.

fun fact

Kem loves 'girls with chubby fingers'. Why not?

Amber

Chyna

Georgia

52 days in the villa

No one could keep Kem and Amber apart

Chloe

Day 52 WINNER!!!

Day 1 Entered the villa

'Don't tell me to slow down, you don't want to go down that motorway with me.'

MEMORABLE MOMENT:

The Bracelet

In the most pre-planned, spur-of-the-moment romantic gesture of all time, Kem presented Amber with an infinity bracelet, which he had bought BEFORE entering the villa. Talk about counting your chicks...

celebrity crush:
CHERYL TWEEDY IN HER PRIME

Don't let her Liam hear you say that.

TYPE ON PAPER:

He'd never had a girlfriend before Amber but he says he's into 'small, tanned, petite and endearing girls' – essentially a female version of himself.

Islander
Uploads

In the villa, phones were used for three main things. Receiving texts, sending sexts and, of course, taking selfies. But because we'd turned the Wi-Fi off, our Islanders were unable to share any of their amazing holiday pictures on social media. Here's a selection of our favourite unseen snaps direct from the Islanders' phones.

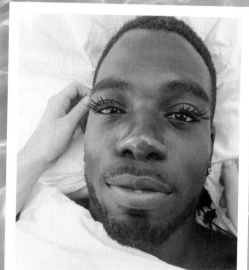

Marcel on the lash
#LashesOnFleek

Staying tight-lipped
#MuggyMike #VillaFillers

Getting the horn on a unicorn!
#BigD #FancyADip

These boobs bite!
#Motherpuckers
#BlazinLove

Bromantic table for two
#BroVibes #BestMan

My main Man-icure
#NailingLife #SingleFile

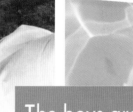

The boys are
all-white!
#WhiteWash

Sun's out, guns out!
#HunksInTrunks #LadsLadsLads

Daddy daycare
#Dummies #TopOfThePops

Sun's out, buns out!
#FullMoon #CheekyGirls

Photobum!!!
#SpotTheAss #StayMuggy

Resting bitch... face
#BeautySleep #LivTheDream

100% your type on paper
#YouWould #FitAs

Get a room
#FlooredHer #SleepingBooty

The calm before the Stormzy!
#GrimeTime #BigForYourBoots

Let's throw this one back
#PlentyOfFish

Bath time at
the villa
#InHotWater
#HottieTub

Say it with... pretzels
#GoAndLoveYourself
#CasaAmor

I LOVE
MYSELF

Girl-on-girl action
#GirlsOnTop
#LoveTriangle

FULL NAME:

Amber
Davies

NICKNAME:

The
Double
Dipper

Scan this QR code
on any smartphone
QR scanner app
to access exclusive
unseen footage of
Amber

Amber

WINNER!!

**Pre-Island
Occupation:**

Part-time waitress/
professional dancer

So basically, she's
a waitress!

celebrity lookalike:

ARIANA
GRANDE

Apparently...
Well, she does
seem like a
*Dangerous
Woman!*

Amber has her nipple pierced.

(Yeah, Nathan! Remember him?)

Nathan

Kem

Amber was quick to trade Harley for Kem

52 days in the villa

Jonny

Harley

KNOWN FOR:

HAVING A LOT OF PAPER

No matter who it was, where they came from or what they looked like, it seemed that every man who entered the villa was Amber's type on paper.

'He's 100 per cent my type on paper.'

MEMORABLE MOMENT:

That Face!!

After a rather tense re-coupling, where Georgia stole her boyfriend Kem, Amber pulled the most meme-able face of all time!

Day 52
WINNER!!!

Day 1
Entered the villa

celebrity crush: CHANNING TATUM

OK, Channing's a great dancer, but can he rap like Kem?

TYPE ON PAPER:

'Short men, tall men, muscly men, skinny men, blonde men, redheaded men, bald men...' Basically, she likes men!

THE ULTIMATE

Love Island Quiz

It was a summer of love, and you lot loved every minute of it, but how much of the series do you really remember? Do you know your originals from your bombshells? Can you remember who broke up and who hooked up? Well, it's time to find out if you're a wise worldie or a mediocre melt with our ultimate *Love Island* quiz! Take it away...

1. Who was Montana initially paired up with?

2. Where in Spain was the 2017 *Love Island* villa?

3. What was the total number of Islanders in BOTH villas this series?

4. What colour are the walls in the Hideaway?

5. What was Marcel's nickname for his 'little friend'?

6. Name the other girl who entered Casa Amor: Chyna, Danielle, Shannen, Ellisha-Jade and...?

7. How many re-couplings were there during the series?

8. Which female Islander had the most partners in the villa?

9. Who came up with the now infamous nickname 'Muggy Mike'?

11. During the white party in the villa, new girl Georgia walked in wearing what colour dress?

12. From start to finish, how many days were the Islanders in the villa?

13. Who did Tyla enter the villa with?

10. How many entries were on Liv's list of things she liked/loved about Chris?

14. BEFORE entering the villa, who did Mike go on a date with as her reward for winning a challenge?

CONTINUED >>>

15. Who was the first girl Chris kissed in the villa?

16. Who were the first people to have sex in the Hideaway?

17. Which two dumped Islanders later returned to the villa?

18. What did Jamie use to spell out 'Happy Bday Cam'?

19. What is Camilla's favourite song?

20. Which girl did Kem kiss in Casa Amor?

21. What did Marcel say his favourite sex position was?

22. Who in the villa was first to hear the rumour about Jess and Mike?

23. Which singer made a cameo appearance in the series?

24. Whose signature catchphrase was, 'D'you know what I mean?'

25. How many birthdays were celebrated in the villa?

26. What was the full name of Chris and Olivia's baby?

27. What animal did Chris famously compare himself to?

28. Which two Islanders performed a roast at the talent show?

29. Who was the surprise final Islander to enter the villa on Day 1?

30. How many of the original line-up made it to the final?

ANSWERS ON PAGE 207 >>>

A Right Roasting

Without being mean, despite the romance and drama we spent a lot of time laughing at our Islanders. But on this occasion we were laughing with them. Amber and Olivia proved themselves to be a brilliant comedy double act when they took the mike (not the muggy one) and performed a devastating stand-up comedy roast about their fellow Islanders.

Get ready for Amber and Olivia to tickle your funny bones...

AMBER: Welcome to the Love Island roast.

OLIVIA: This is something that you've all been waiting for... Marce, I feel like we're going to take some words right out of your mouth.

AMBER: That's only if you haven't already written it to Gab in a text.
Who's looking forward to Mon and Gab's collaboration tonight?

OLIVIA: Watching these two up here pretending to like each other is almost as fake as my t*ts.
Then we've got Al. David Beckham, I see it. Very good looking, but a little bit like watching paint dry.

AMBER: Camilla and Jamie!

OLIVIA: I hope you'll humour us with a bit of light-hearted banter.

AMBER: We know it's not world politics.

OLIVIA: But we thought you were getting a bit cold up there on your pedestals.

AMBER: So now, moving on to our little babies! [Chris and Kem]

OLIVIA: The main event, guys! We're glad you could take a little time out from rooting around each other's pubes to be here.

AMBER: And convincing each other that you're going to have a rap career on the outside world...

Good effort, girls, you had the whole villa and everyone at home in absolute stitches. As for your predictions about Chris and Kem's rap career – only time will tell...

ANSWERS

1. Dom
2. Mallorca
3. 32
4. White
5. Rocky B
6. Amelia
7. Eight
8. Montana
9. Chris
10. Ten
11. Red
12. 52
13. Simon
14. Tyne-Lexy
15. Chloe
16. Dom and Jess
17. Sam and Mike
18. Toast and avocados
19. 'Africa' by Toto
20. Chyna
21. Superman Doggy
22. Gabby
23. Stormzy
24. Craig
25. Two – Jess's and Camilla's
26. Cash Hughes
27. Polar bear
28. Amber and Olivia
29. Jess
30. Five – Marcel, Camilla, Olivia, Kem and Amber

Acknowledgements

The publishers would like to thank Steve Parry and Sabah Ahmed for their fantastic text and endless enthusiasm. We'd also like to thank Kevin O'Brien, Shirley Patton, Richard Cowles and Andy Cadman at ITV for their support throughout. Our `panel of experts' were invaluable on occasion, particularly Faye Lehane, Ella Parsons, Nell Warner, Nicole Brown, Matt Grindon and Anna Gruber. This book could not have happened without the tireless efforts of our Designer Abi Read, Editor Zia Mattocks, Assistant Editor Ellie Corbett and Senior Production Manager Peter Hunt.